Reach Your Potential

IN THIS SPECIAL ARTICLE COLLECTION:

Harvard Business Review

www.hbrreprints.org

BEST OF HBR 1980

If you forge ties with your boss based on mutual respect and understanding, both of you will be more effective.

Managing Your Boss

by John J. Gabarro and John P. Kotter

Included with this full-text *Harvard Business Review* article:

Reprint R0501J

Managing Your Boss

The Idea in Brief

Managing our *bosses*? Isn't that merely manipulation? Corporate cozying up? Out-and-out apple polishing? In fact, we manage our bosses for very good reasons: to get resources to do the best job, not only for ourselves, but for our bosses and our companies as well. We actively pursue a healthy and productive working relationship based on mutual respect and understanding—understanding our own and our bosses' strengths, weaknesses, goals, work styles, and needs. Here's what can happen when we don't:

▶ Example:

A new president with a formal work style replaced someone who'd been looser, more intuitive. The new president preferred written reports and structured meetings. One of his managers found this too controlling. He seldom sent background information, and was often blindsided by unanticipated questions. His boss found their meetings inefficient and frustrating. The manager had to resign.

In contrast, here's how another manager's sensitivity to this same boss's style really paid off:

▶ Example:

This manager identified the kinds and frequency of information the president wanted. He sent ahead background reports and discussion agendas. The result? Highly productive meetings and even more innovative problem solving than with his previous boss.

Managers often don't realize how much their bosses depend on them. They need cooperation, reliability, and honesty from their direct reports. Many managers also don't realize how much *they* depend on their bosses—for links to the rest of the organization, for setting priorities, and for obtaining critical resources.

Recognizing this mutual dependence, effective managers seek out information about the boss's concerns and are sensitive to his work style. They also understand how their own attitudes toward authority can sabotage the relationship. Some see the boss as the enemy and fight him at every turn; others are overly compliant, viewing the boss as an all-wise parent.

The Idea in Practice

You can benefit from this mutual dependence and develop a very productive relationship with your boss by focusing on:

- **compatible work styles**. Bosses process information differently. "Listeners" prefer to be briefed in person so they can ask questions. "Readers" want to process written information first, and then meet to discuss.

Decision-making styles also vary. Some bosses are highly involved. Touch base with them frequently. Others prefer to delegate. Inform them about important decisions you've already made.

- **mutual expectations**. Don't passively assume you know what the boss expects. Find out. With some bosses, write detailed outlines of your work for their approval. With others, carefully planned discussions are key.

Also, communicate *your* expectations to find out if they are realistic. Persuade the boss to accept the most important ones.

- **information flow**. Managers typically underestimate what their bosses need to know—and what they *do* know. Keep the boss informed through processes that fit his style. Be forthright about both good and bad news.

- **dependability and honesty**. Trustworthy subordinates only make promises they can keep and don't shade the truth or play down difficult issues.

- **good use of time and resources**. Don't waste your boss's time with trivial issues. Selectively draw on his time and resources to meet the most important goals—yours, his, and the company's.

If you forge ties with your boss based on mutual respect and understanding, both of you will be more effective.

BEST OF HBR 1980

Managing Your Boss

by John J. Gabarro and John P. Kotter

A quarter-century ago, John Gabarro and John Kotter introduced a powerful new lens through which to view the manager–boss relationship: one that recognized the mutual dependence of the participants.

The fact is, bosses need cooperation, reliability, and honesty from their direct reports. Managers, for their part, rely on bosses for making connections with the rest of the company, for setting priorities, and for obtaining critical resources. If the relationship between you and your boss is rocky, then it is you who must begin to manage it. When you take the time to cultivate a productive working relationship—by understanding your boss's strengths and weaknesses, priorities, and work style—everyone wins.

In the 25 years since it was published, this article has truly improved the practice of management. Its simple yet powerful advice has changed the way people work, enhanced countless manager–boss relationships, and improved the performance of corporations in ways that show up on the bottom line. Over the years, it has become a staple at business schools and corporate training programs worldwide.

To many people, the phrase "managing your boss" may sound unusual or suspicious. Because of the traditional top-down emphasis in most organizations, it is not obvious why you need to manage relationships upward—unless, of course, you would do so for personal or political reasons. But we are not referring to political maneuvering or to apple polishing. We are using the term to mean the process of consciously working with your superior to obtain the best possible results for you, your boss, and the company.

Recent studies suggest that effective managers take time and effort to manage not only relationships with their subordinates but also those with their bosses. These studies also show that this essential aspect of management is sometimes ignored by otherwise talented and aggressive managers. Indeed, some managers who actively and effectively supervise subordinates, products, markets, and technologies assume an almost passively reactive stance vis-à-vis their bosses. Such a stance almost always hurts them and their companies.

If you doubt the importance of managing your relationship with your boss or how difficult it is to do so effectively, consider for a moment the following sad but telling story:

Frank Gibbons was an acknowledged manufacturing genius in his industry and, by any profitability standard, a very effective executive. In 1973, his strengths propelled him into the position of vice president of manufacturing for the second largest and most profitable company in its industry. Gibbons was not, however, a good manager of people. He knew this, as did others in his company and his industry. Recognizing this weakness, the president made sure that those who reported to Gibbons were good at working with people and could compensate for his limitations. The arrangement worked well.

In 1975, Philip Bonnevie was promoted into a position reporting to Gibbons. In keeping with the previous pattern, the president selected Bonnevie because he had an excellent track record and a reputation for being good with people. In making that selection, however, the president neglected to notice that, in his rapid rise through the organization, Bonnevie had always had good-to-excellent bosses. He had never been forced to manage a relationship with a difficult boss. In retrospect, Bonnevie admits he had never thought that managing his boss was a part of his job.

Fourteen months after he started working for Gibbons, Bonnevie was fired. During that same quarter, the company reported a net loss for the first time in seven years. Many of those who were close to these events say that they don't really understand what happened. This much is known, however: While the company was bringing out a major new product—a process that required sales, engineering, and manufacturing groups to coordinate decisions very carefully—a whole series of misunderstandings and bad feelings developed between Gibbons and Bonnevie.

For example, Bonnevie claims Gibbons was aware of and had accepted Bonnevie's decision to use a new type of machinery to make the new product; Gibbons swears he did not. Furthermore, Gibbons claims he made it clear to Bonnevie that the introduction of the product

was too important to the company in the short run to take any major risks.

As a result of such misunderstandings, planning went awry: A new manufacturing plant was built that could not produce the new product designed by engineering, in the volume desired by sales, at a cost agreed on by the executive committee. Gibbons blamed Bonnevie for the mistake. Bonnevie blamed Gibbons.

Of course, one could argue that the problem here was caused by Gibbons's inability to manage his subordinates. But one can make just as strong a case that the problem was related to Bonnevie's inability to manage his boss. Remember, Gibbons was not having difficulty with any other subordinates. Moreover, given the personal price paid by Bonnevie (being fired and having his reputation within the industry severely tarnished), there was little consolation in saying the problem was that Gibbons was poor at managing subordinates. Everyone already knew that.

We believe that the situation could have turned out differently had Bonnevie been more adept at understanding Gibbons and at managing his relationship with him. In this case, an inability to manage upward was unusually costly. The company lost $2 million to $5 million, and Bonnevie's career was, at least temporarily, disrupted. Many less costly cases similar to this probably occur regularly in all major corporations, and the cumulative effect can be very destructive.

Misreading the Boss–Subordinate Relationship

People often dismiss stories like the one we just related as being merely cases of personality conflict. Because two people can on occasion be psychologically or temperamentally incapable of working together, this can be an apt description. But more often, we have found, a personality conflict is only a part of the problem—sometimes a very small part.

Bonnevie did not just have a different personality from Gibbons, he also made or had unrealistic assumptions and expectations about the very nature of boss–subordinate relationships. Specifically, he did not recognize that his relationship to Gibbons involved *mutual dependence* between two *fallible* human beings. Failing to recognize this, a manager typically either avoids trying to manage his or her relationship with a boss or manages it ineffectively.

John J. Gabarro is the UPS Foundation Professor of Human Resource Management at Harvard Business School in Boston. Now retired, **John P. Kotter** was the Konosuke Matsushita Professor of Leadership at Harvard Business School.

Some people behave as if their bosses were not very dependent on them. They fail to see how much the boss needs their help and co-operation to do his or her job effectively. These people refuse to acknowledge that the boss can be severely hurt by their actions and needs cooperation, dependability, and honesty from them.

Some people see themselves as not very dependent on their bosses. They gloss over how much help and information they need from the boss in order to perform their own jobs well. This superficial view is particularly damaging when a manager's job and decisions affect other parts of the organization, as was the case in Bonnevie's situation. A manager's immediate boss can play a critical role in linking the manager to the rest of the organization, making sure the manager's priorities are consistent with organizational needs, and in securing the resources the manager needs to perform well. Yet some managers need to see themselves as practically self-sufficient, as not needing the critical information and resources a boss can supply.

Many managers, like Bonnevie, assume that the boss will magically know what information or help their subordinates need and provide it to them. Certainly, some bosses do an excellent job of caring for their subordinates in this way, but for a manager to expect that from all bosses is dangerously unrealistic. A more reasonable expectation for managers to have is that modest help will be forthcoming. After all, bosses are only human. Most really effective managers accept this fact and assume primary responsibility for their own careers and development. They make a point of seeking the information and help they need to do a job instead of waiting for their bosses to provide it.

In light of the foregoing, it seems to us that managing a situation of mutual dependence among fallible human beings requires the following:

1. You have a good understanding of the other person and yourself, especially regarding strengths, weaknesses, work styles, and needs.

2. You use this information to develop and manage a healthy working relationship—one that is compatible with both people's work styles and assets, is characterized by mutual expectations, and meets the most critical needs of the other person.

This combination is essentially what we have found highly effective managers doing.

Understanding the Boss

Managing your boss requires that you gain an understanding of the boss and his or her context, as well as your own situation. All managers do this to some degree, but many are not thorough enough.

At a minimum, you need to appreciate your boss's goals and pressures, his or her strengths and weaknesses. What are your boss's organizational and personal objectives, and what are his or her pressures, especially those from his or her own boss and others at the same level? What are your boss's long suits and blind spots? What is the preferred style of working? Does your boss like to get information through memos, formal meetings, or phone calls? Does he or she thrive on conflict or try to minimize it? Without this information, a manager is flying blind when dealing with the boss, and unnecessary conflicts, misunderstandings, and problems are inevitable.

In one situation we studied, a top-notch marketing manager with a superior performance record was hired into a company as a vice president "to straighten out the marketing and sales problems." The company, which was having financial difficulties, had recently been acquired by a larger corporation. The president was eager to turn it around and gave the new marketing vice president free rein—at least initially. Based on his previous experience, the new vice president correctly diagnosed that greater market share was needed for the company and that strong product management was required to bring that about. Following that logic, he made a number of pricing decisions aimed at increasing high-volume business.

When margins declined and the financial situation did not improve, however, the president increased pressure on the new vice president. Believing that the situation would eventually correct itself as the company gained back market share, the vice president resisted the pressure.

When by the second quarter, margins and profits had still failed to improve, the president took direct control over all pricing decisions and put all items on a set level of margin, regardless of volume. The new vice president began to find himself shut out by

At a minimum, you need to appreciate your boss's goals and pressures. Without this information, you are flying blind, and problems are inevitable.

the president, and their relationship deteriorated. In fact, the vice president found the president's behavior bizarre. Unfortunately, the president's new pricing scheme also failed to increase margins, and by the fourth quarter, both the president and the vice president were fired.

What the new vice president had not known until it was too late was that improving marketing and sales had been only *one* of the president's goals. His most immediate goal had been to make the company more profitable—quickly.

Nor had the new vice president known that his boss was invested in this short-term priority for personal as well as business reasons. The president had been a strong advocate of the acquisition within the parent company, and his personal credibility was at stake.

The vice president made three basic errors. He took information supplied to him at face value, he made assumptions in areas where he had no information, and—what was most damaging—he never actively tried to clarify what his boss's objectives were. As a result, he ended up taking actions that were actually at odds with the president's priorities and objectives.

Managers who work effectively with their bosses do not behave this way. They seek out information about the boss's goals and problems and pressures. They are alert for opportunities to question the boss and others around him or her to test their assumptions. They pay attention to clues in the boss's behavior. Although it is imperative that they do this especially when they begin working with a new boss, effective managers also do this on an ongoing basis because they recognize that priorities and concerns change.

Being sensitive to a boss's work style can be crucial, especially when the boss is new. For example, a new president who was organized and formal in his approach replaced a man who was informal and intuitive. The new president worked best when he had written reports. He also preferred formal meetings with set agendas.

One of his division managers realized this need and worked with the new president to identify the kinds and frequency of information and reports that the president wanted. This manager also made a point of sending background information and brief agendas ahead of time for their discussions. He found that with this type of preparation their meetings were very useful. Another interesting result was, he found that with adequate preparation his new boss was even more effective at brainstorming problems than his more informal and intuitive predecessor had been.

In contrast, another division manager never fully understood how the new boss's work style differed from that of his predecessor. To the degree that he did sense it, he experienced it as too much control. As a result, he seldom sent the new president the background information he needed, and the president never felt fully prepared for meetings with the manager. In fact, the president spent much of the time when they met trying to get information that he felt he should have had earlier. The boss experienced these meetings as frustrating and inefficient, and the subordinate often found himself thrown off guard by the questions that the president asked. Ultimately, this division manager resigned.

The difference between the two division managers just described was not so much one of ability or even adaptability. Rather, one of the men was more sensitive to his boss's work style and to the implications of his boss's needs than the other was.

Understanding Yourself

The boss is only one-half of the relationship. You are the other half, as well as the part over which you have more direct control. Developing an effective working relationship requires, then, that you know your own needs, strengths and weaknesses, and personal style.

You are not going to change either your basic personality structure or that of your boss. But you can become aware of what it is about you that impedes or facilitates working with your boss and, with that awareness, take actions that make the relationship more effective.

For example, in one case we observed, a manager and his superior ran into problems whenever they disagreed. The boss's typical response was to harden his position and overstate it. The manager's reaction was then to raise the ante and intensify the forcefulness of his argument. In doing this, he channeled his anger into sharpening his attacks on the logical fallacies he saw in his boss's assumptions. His boss in turn would become even more adamant about holding his original position. Predictably, this escalating cycle resulted in the subordinate avoiding whenever possible any topic of potential conflict with his boss.

In discussing this problem with his peers, the manager discovered that his reaction to the boss was typical of how he generally reacted to counterarguments—but with a difference. His response would overwhelm his peers but not his boss. Because his attempts to discuss this problem with his boss were unsuccessful, he concluded that the only way to change the situation was to deal with his own instinctive reactions. Whenever the two reached an impasse, he would check his own impatience and suggest that they break up and think about it before getting together again. Usually when they renewed their discussion, they had digested their differences and were more able to work them through.

Gaining this level of self-awareness and acting on it are difficult but not impossible. For example, by reflecting over his past experiences, a young manager learned that he was not very good at dealing with difficult and emotional issues where people were involved. Because he disliked those issues and realized that his instinctive responses to them were seldom very good, he developed a habit of touching base with his boss whenever such a problem arose. Their discussions always surfaced ideas and approaches the manager had not considered. In many cases, they also identified specific actions the boss could take to help.

Although a superior–subordinate relationship is one of mutual dependence, it is also one in which the subordinate is typically more dependent on the boss than the other way around. This dependence inevitably results in the subordinate feeling a certain degree of frustration, sometimes anger, when his actions or options are constrained by his boss's decisions. This is a normal part of life and occurs in the best of relationships. The way in which a manager handles these frustrations largely depends on his or her predisposition toward dependence on authority figures.

Some people's instinctive reaction under these circumstances is to resent the boss's authority and to rebel against the boss's decisions. Sometimes a person will escalate a conflict beyond what is appropriate. Seeing the boss almost as an institutional enemy, this type of manager will often, without being conscious of it, fight with the boss just for the sake of

fighting. The subordinate's reactions to being constrained are usually strong and sometimes impulsive. He or she sees the boss as someone who, by virtue of the role, is a hindrance to progress, an obstacle to be circumvented or at best tolerated.

Psychologists call this pattern of reactions counterdependent behavior. Although a counterdependent person is difficult for most superiors to manage and usually has a history of strained relationships with superiors, this sort of manager is apt to have even more trouble with a boss who tends to be directive or authoritarian. When the manager acts on his or her negative feelings, often in subtle and nonverbal ways, the boss sometimes does become the enemy. Sensing the subordinate's latent hostility, the boss will lose trust in the subordinate or his or her judgment and then behave even less openly.

Paradoxically, a manager with this type of predisposition is often a good manager of his or her own people. He or she will many times go out of the way to get support for them and will not hesitate to go to bat for them.

At the other extreme are managers who swallow their anger and behave in a very compliant fashion when the boss makes what they know to be a poor decision. These managers will agree with the boss even when a disagreement might be welcome or when the boss would easily alter a decision if given more information. Because they bear no relationship to the specific situation at hand, their responses are as much an overreaction as those of counterdependent managers. Instead of seeing the boss as an enemy, these people deny their anger—the other extreme—and tend to see the boss as if he or she were an all-wise parent who should know best, should take responsibility for their careers, train them in all they need to know, and protect them from overly ambitious peers.

Both counterdependence and overdependence lead managers to hold unrealistic views of what a boss is. Both views ignore that bosses, like everyone else, are imperfect and fallible. They don't have unlimited time, encyclopedic knowledge, or extrasensory perception; nor are they evil enemies. They have their own pressures and concerns that are sometimes at odds with the wishes of the subordinate—and often for good reason.

Altering predispositions toward authority,

Bosses, like everyone else, are imperfect and fallible. They don't have unlimited time, encyclopedic knowledge, or extrasensory perception; nor are they evil enemies.

especially at the extremes, is almost impossible without intensive psychotherapy (psychoanalytic theory and research suggest that such predispositions are deeply rooted in a person's personality and upbringing). However, an awareness of these extremes and the range between them can be very useful in understanding where your own predispositions fall and what the implications are for how you tend to behave in relation to your boss.

If you believe, on the one hand, that you have some tendencies toward counterdependence, you can understand and even predict what your reactions and overreactions are likely to be. If, on the other hand, you believe you have some tendencies toward overdependence, you might question the extent to which your overcompliance or inability to confront real differences may be making both you and your boss less effective.

Developing and Managing the Relationship

With a clear understanding of both your boss

and yourself, you can *usually* establish a way of working together that fits both of you, that is characterized by unambiguous mutual expectations, and that helps you both be more productive and effective. The "Checklist for Managing Your Boss" summarizes some things such a relationship consists of. Following are a few more.

Compatible Work Styles. Above all else, a good working relationship with a boss accommodates differences in work style. For example, in one situation we studied, a manager (who had a relatively good relationship with his superior) realized that during meetings his boss would often become inattentive and sometimes brusque. The subordinate's own style tended to be discursive and exploratory. He would often digress from the topic at hand to deal with background factors, alternative approaches, and so forth. His boss preferred to discuss problems with a minimum of background detail and became impatient and distracted whenever his subordinate digressed from the immediate issue.

Recognizing this difference in style, the manager became terser and more direct during meetings with his boss. To help himself do this, before meetings, he would develop brief agendas that he used as a guide. Whenever he felt that a digression was needed, he explained why. This small shift in his own style made these meetings more effective and far less frustrating for both of them.

Subordinates can adjust their styles in response to their bosses' preferred method for receiving information. Peter Drucker divides bosses into "listeners" and "readers." Some bosses like to get information in report form so they can read and study it. Others work better with information and reports presented in person so they can ask questions. As Drucker points out, the implications are obvious. If your boss is a listener, you brief him or her in person, *then* follow it up with a memo. If your boss is a reader, you cover important items or proposals in a memo or report, *then* discuss them.

Other adjustments can be made according to a boss's decision-making style. Some bosses prefer to be involved in decisions and problems as they arise. These are high-involvement managers who like to keep their hands on the pulse of the operation. Usually their needs (and your own) are best satisfied if you touch

Checklist for Managing Your Boss

Make sure you understand your boss and his or her context, including:

❑ Goals and objectives

❑ Pressures

❑ Strengths, weaknesses, blind spots

❑ Preferred work style

Assess yourself and your needs, including:

❑ Strengths and weaknesses

❑ Personal style

❑ Predisposition toward dependence on authority figures

Develop and maintain a relationship that:

❑ Fits both your needs and styles

❑ Is characterized by mutual expectations

❑ Keeps your boss informed

❑ Is based on dependability and honesty

❑ Selectively uses your boss's time and resources

base with them on an ad hoc basis. A boss who has a need to be involved will become involved one way or another, so there are advantages to including him or her at your initiative. Other bosses prefer to delegate—they don't want to be involved. They expect you to come to them with major problems and inform them about any important changes.

Creating a compatible relationship also involves drawing on each other's strengths and making up for each other's weaknesses. Because he knew that the boss—the vice president of engineering—was not very good at monitoring his employees' problems, one manager we studied made a point of doing it himself. The stakes were high: The engineers and technicians were all union members, the company worked on a customer-contract basis, and the company had recently experienced a serious strike.

The manager worked closely with his boss, along with people in the scheduling department and the personnel office, to make sure that potential problems were avoided. He also developed an informal arrangement through which his boss would review with him any proposed changes in personnel or assignment policies before taking action. The boss valued his advice and credited his subordinate for improving both the performance of the division and the labor–management climate.

Mutual Expectations. The subordinate who passively assumes that he or she knows what the boss expects is in for trouble. Of course, some superiors will spell out their expectations very explicitly and in great detail. But most do not. And although many corporations have systems that provide a basis for communicating expectations (such as formal planning processes, career planning reviews, and performance appraisal reviews), these systems never work perfectly. Also, between these formal reviews, expectations invariably change.

Ultimately, the burden falls on the subordinate to find out what the boss's expectations are. They can be both broad (such as what kinds of problems the boss wishes to be informed about and when) as well as very specific (such things as when a particular project should be completed and what kinds of information the boss needs in the interim).

Getting a boss who tends to be vague or not explicit to express expectations can be difficult. But effective managers find ways to get that in-

formation. Some will draft a detailed memo covering key aspects of their work and then send it to their boss for approval. They then follow this up with a face-to-face discussion in which they go over each item in the memo. A discussion like this will often surface virtually all of the boss's expectations.

Other effective managers will deal with an inexplicit boss by initiating an ongoing series of informal discussions about "good management" and "our objectives." Still others find useful information more indirectly through those who used to work for the boss and through the formal planning systems in which the boss makes commitments to his or her own superior. Which approach you choose, of course, should depend on your understanding of your boss's style.

Developing a workable set of mutual expectations also requires that you communicate your own expectations to the boss, find out if they are realistic, and influence the boss to accept the ones that are important to you. Being able to influence the boss to value your expectations can be particularly important if the boss is an overachiever. Such a boss will often set unrealistically high standards that need to be brought into line with reality.

A Flow of Information. How much information a boss needs about what a subordinate is doing will vary significantly depending on the boss's style, the situation he or she is in, and the confidence the boss has in the subordinate. But it is not uncommon for a boss to need more information than the subordinate would naturally supply or for the subordinate to think the boss knows more than he or she really does. Effective managers recognize that they probably underestimate what their bosses need to know and make sure they find ways to keep them informed through processes that fit their styles.

Managing the flow of information upward is particularly difficult if the boss does not like to hear about problems. Although many people would deny it, bosses often give off signals that they want to hear only good news. They show great displeasure—usually nonverbally—when someone tells them about a problem. Ignoring individual achievement, they may even evaluate more favorably subordinates who do not bring problems to them.

Nevertheless, for the good of the organization, the boss, and the subordinate, a superior

Some superiors spell out their expectations very explicitly. But most do not. Ultimately, the burden falls on the subordinate to find out what the boss's expectations are.

needs to hear about failures as well as successes. Some subordinates deal with a good-news-only boss by finding indirect ways to get the necessary information to him or her, such as a management information system. Others see to it that potential problems, whether in the form of good surprises or bad news, are communicated immediately.

Dependability and Honesty. Few things are more disabling to a boss than a subordinate on whom he cannot depend, whose work he cannot trust. Almost no one is intentionally undependable, but many managers are inadvertently so because of oversight or uncertainty about the boss's priorities. A commitment to an optimistic delivery date may please a superior in the short term but become a source of displeasure if not honored. It's difficult for a boss to rely on a subordinate who repeatedly slips deadlines. As one president (describing a subordinate) put it: "I'd rather he be more consistent even if he delivered fewer peak successes—at least I could rely on him."

Nor are many managers intentionally dishonest with their bosses. But it is easy to shade the truth and play down issues. Current concerns often become future surprise problems. It's almost impossible for bosses to work effectively if they cannot rely on a fairly accurate reading from their subordinates. Because it undermines credibility, dishonesty is perhaps the most troubling trait a subordinate can have. Without a basic level of trust, a boss feels compelled to check all of a subordinate's decisions, which makes it difficult to delegate.

Good Use of Time and Resources. Your boss is probably as limited in his or her store of time, energy, and influence as you are. Every request you make of your boss uses up some of these resources, so it's wise to draw on these resources selectively. This may sound obvious, but many managers use up their boss's time (and some of their own credibility) over relatively trivial issues.

One vice president went to great lengths to get his boss to fire a meddlesome secretary in another department. His boss had to use considerable influence to do it. Understandably, the head of the other department was not pleased. Later, when the vice president wanted to tackle more important problems, he ran into trouble. By using up blue chips on a relatively trivial issue, he had made it difficult for him and his boss to meet more important goals.

No doubt, some subordinates will resent that on top of all their other duties, they also need to take time and energy to manage their relationships with their bosses. Such managers fail to realize the importance of this activity and how it can simplify their jobs by eliminating potentially severe problems. Effective managers recognize that this part of their work is legitimate. Seeing themselves as ultimately responsible for what they achieve in an organization, they know they need to establish and manage relationships with everyone on whom they depend—and that includes the boss.

Reprint R0501J
To order, see the next page
or call 800-988-0886 or 617-783-7500
or go to www.hbrreprints.org

Managing Your Boss

Further Reading

ARTICLES

The Subordinate's Predicaments
by Eric H. Neilsen and Jan Gypen
Harvard Business Review
September–October 1979
Product no. 79507

This article provides the psychological backdrop for "Managing Your Boss," stressing again how important it is to be an effective subordinate—just as important as being an effective supervisor. "Managing Your Boss" presents the concept primarily from the subordinate's perspective; this article includes the boss's as well.

It stresses that the supervisor's power drives the subordinate to adopt self-protective behaviors that undermine performance. Drawing upon the ideas of psychologist Erik Erikson, the authors describe eight dilemmas subordinates must resolve in dealing with supervisors. They also suggest how supervisors can help, using introspection, empathy, and preparedness.

The Manager: Master and Servant of Power
by Fernando Bartolomé and André Laurent
Harvard Business Review
November–December 1986
Product no. 86603

This article, like "The Subordinate's Predicaments," focuses both on the boss and the direct report—the "master" and the "servant" in work relationships. It highlights this irony: while most managers function as both supervisors and subordinates, they often are unable to put themselves in the others' shoes. This exacerbates the conflicts and misunderstandings that arise because of power differences. But there are steps managers can take to harmonize these often opposing perspectives. The key is to link the two roles to draw on the insights gained from working with those from above as well as those from below them in the organizational hierarchy. The article rein-

forces the concepts of "Managing Your Boss" by making specific suggestions for how direct reports can strengthen their relationships with higher-ups.

The Set-Up-to-Fail Syndrome
by Jean-François Manzoni and Jean-Louis Barsoux
Harvard Business Review
March–April 1998
Product no. 861X

This article expands the repertoire of ways to pursue healthy and productive work relationships based on mutual respect and understanding, as stressed in "Managing Your Boss." It puts the focus on the manager and the role he plays in employees' poor performance. When an employee performs poorly, managers typically assume that the fault lies entirely with the employee. The authors take a different view. In a reversal of the Pygmalion effect, they argue, employees perceived as weak performers proceed to live *down* to their manager's low expectations for them. This costly syndrome, however, is neither irreversible nor inevitable. The authors describe an intervention to break the pattern and suggest how managers can avoid setting up their employees to fail in the first place.

Harvard Business Review ❦

To Order

For *Harvard Business Review* reprints and subscriptions, call 800-988-0886 or 617-783-7500. Go to www.hbrreprints.org

For customized and quantity orders of *Harvard Business Review* article reprints, call 617-783-7626, or e-mail customizations@hbsp.harvard.edu

www.hbrreprints.org

MANAGING YOURSELF

Successful leaders have a nose for opportunity and a knack for knowing whom to tap to get things done. These qualities depend on a set of strategic networking skills that nonleaders rarely possess.

How Leaders Create and Use Networks

by Herminia Ibarra and Mark Hunter

Included with this full-text *Harvard Business Review* article:

Reprint R0701C

How Leaders Create and Use Networks

The Idea in Brief

What separates successful leaders from the rest of the pack? Networking: creating a tissue of personal contacts to provide the support, feedback, and resources needed to get things done.

Yet many leaders avoid networking. Some think they don't have time for it. Others disdain it as manipulative.

To succeed as a leader, Ibarra and Hunter recommend building three types of networks:

- **Operational**—people you need to accomplish your assigned, routine tasks.

- **Personal**—kindred spirits outside your organization who can help you with personal advancement.

- **Strategic**—people outside your control who will enable you to reach key organizational objectives.

You need all three types of networks. But to *really* succeed, you must master strategic networking—by interacting regularly with people who can open your eyes to new business opportunities and help you capitalize on them. Build your strategic network, and burnish your own—and your company's—performance.

The Idea in Practice

The most effective leaders understand the differences among the three types of networks and how to build them.

	Operational network	Personal network	Strategic network
Network's purpose	Getting work done efficiently	Develop professional skills through coaching and mentoring; exchange important referrals and needed outside information.	Figure out future priorities and challenges; get stakeholder support for them.
How to find network members	Identify individuals who can block or support a project.	Participate in professional associations, alumni groups, clubs, and personal-interest communities.	Identify lateral and vertical relationships with other functional and business-unit managers—people outside your immediate control—who can help you determine how your role and contribution fit into the overall picture.

LEVERAGING YOUR NETWORKS

Networking takes work. To lessen the pain and increase the gain:

- **Mind your mind-set.** Accept that networking is one of the most important requirements of a leadership role. To overcome any qualms about it, identify a person you respect who networks effectively and ethically. Observe how he or she uses networks to accomplish goals.

- **Reallocate your time.** Master the art of delegation, to liberate time you can then spend on cultivating networks.

- **Establish connections.** Create reasons for interacting with people outside your function or organization; for instance, by taking advantage of social interests to set the stage for addressing strategic concerns.

▶ Example:
An investment banker invited key clients to the theatre (a passion of hers) several times a year. Through these events, she developed her own business *and* learned things about her clients' companies that gener-

ated business and ideas for other divisions in her firm.

- **Give and take continually.** Don't wait until you really need something badly to ask for a favor from a network member. Instead, take every opportunity to give to—and receive from—people in your networks, whether you need help or not.

Successful leaders have a nose for opportunity and a knack for knowing whom to tap to get things done. These qualities depend on a set of strategic networking skills that nonleaders rarely possess.

MANAGING YOURSELF

How Leaders Create and Use Networks

by Herminia Ibarra and Mark Hunter

When Henrik Balmer became the production manager and a board member of a newly bought-out cosmetics firm, improving his network was the last thing on his mind. The main problem he faced was time: Where would he find the hours to guide his team through a major upgrade of the production process and then think about strategic issues like expanding the business? The only way he could carve out time and still get home to his family at a decent hour was to lock himself—literally—in his office. Meanwhile, there were day-to-day issues to resolve, like a recurring conflict with his sales director over custom orders that compromised production efficiency. Networking, which Henrik defined as the unpleasant task of trading favors with strangers, was a luxury he could not afford. But when a new acquisition was presented at a board meeting without his input, he abruptly realized he was out of the loop—not just inside the company, but outside, too—at a moment when his future in the company was at stake.

Henrik's case is not unusual. Over the past two years, we have been following a cohort of 30 managers making their way through what we call the leadership transition, an inflection point in their careers that challenges them to rethink both themselves and their roles. In the process, we've found that networking—creating a fabric of personal contacts who will provide support, feedback, insight, resources, and information—is simultaneously one of the most self-evident and one of the most dreaded developmental challenges that aspiring leaders must address.

Their discomfort is understandable. Typically, managers rise through the ranks by dint of a strong command of the technical elements of their jobs and a nose-to-the-grindstone focus on accomplishing their teams' objectives. When challenged to move beyond their functional specialties and address strategic issues facing the overall business, many managers do not immediately grasp that this will involve relational—not analytical—tasks. Nor do they easily understand that exchanges and interactions with a diverse array of current and potential stakeholders are not distractions from their "real work" but are actually at the heart of their new leadership roles.

Like Henrik (whose identity we've disguised, along with all the other managers we describe here), a majority of the managers we work with say that they find networking insincere or manipulative—at best, an elegant way of using people. Not surprisingly, for every manager who instinctively constructs and maintains a useful network, we see several who struggle to overcome this innate resistance. Yet the alternative to networking is to fail—either in reaching for a leadership position or in succeeding at it.

Watching our emerging leaders approach this daunting task, we discovered that three distinct but interdependent forms of networking— *operational, personal,* and *strategic*—played a vital role in their transitions. The first helped them manage current internal responsibilities, the second boosted their personal development, and the third opened their eyes to new business directions and the stakeholders they would need to enlist. While our managers differed in how well they pursued operational and personal networking, we discovered that almost all of them underutilized strategic networking. In this article, we describe key features of each networking form (summarized in the exhibit "The Three Forms of Networking") and, using our managers' experiences, explain how a three-pronged networking strategy can become part and parcel of a new leader's development plan.

Operational Networking

All managers need to build good working relationships with the people who can help them do their jobs. The number and breadth of people involved can be impressive—such operational networks include not only direct reports and superiors but also peers within an operational unit, other internal players with the power to block or support a project, and key outsiders such as suppliers, distributors, and customers. The purpose of this type of networking is to ensure coordination and cooperation among people who have to know and trust one another in order to accomplish their immediate tasks. That isn't always easy, but it is relatively straightforward, because the task provides focus and a clear criterion for membership in the network: Either you're

necessary to the job and helping to get it done, or you're not.

Although operational networking was the form that came most naturally to the managers we studied, nearly every one had important blind spots regarding people and groups they depended on to make things happen. In one case, Alistair, an accounting manager who worked in an entrepreneurial firm with several hundred employees, was suddenly promoted by the company's founder to financial director and given a seat on the board. He was both the youngest and the least-experienced board member, and his instinctive response to these new responsibilities was to reestablish his functional credentials. Acting on a hint from the founder that the company might go public, Alistair undertook a reorganization of the accounting department that would enable the books to withstand close scrutiny. Alistair succeeded brilliantly in upgrading his team's capabilities, but he missed the fact that only a minority of the seven-person board shared the founder's ambition. A year into Alistair's tenure, discussion about whether to take the company public polarized the board, and he discovered that all that time cleaning up the books might have been better spent sounding out his codirectors.

One of the problems with an exclusive reliance on operational networks is that they are usually geared toward meeting objectives as assigned, not toward asking the strategic question, "What *should* we be doing?" By the same token, managers do not exercise as much personal choice in assembling operational relationships as they do in weaving personal and strategic networks, because to a large extent the right relationships are prescribed by the job and organizational structure. Thus, most operational networking occurs within an organization, and ties are determined in large part by routine, short-term demands. Relationships formed with outsiders, such as board members, customers, and regulators, are directly task-related and tend to be bounded and constrained by demands determined at a higher level. Of course, an individual manager can choose to deepen and develop the ties to different extents, and all managers exercise discretion over who gets priority attention. It's the quality of relationships—the rapport and mutual trust—that gives an operational network its power. Nonetheless, the substantial

Herminia Ibarra (herminia.ibarra@ insead.edu) is the Insead Chaired Professor of Organizational Behavior at Insead in Fontainebleau, France, where she also directs the Leadership Transition, an executive program for managers moving into broader leadership roles. Her most recent book is *Working Identity: Unconventional Strategies for Reinventing Your Career* (Harvard Business School Press, 2003). **Mark Hunter** (mark.hunter@insead.edu) is an investigative journalist and an adjunct professor of communications at Insead. He is the author of *The Passions of Men: Work and Love in the Age of Stress* (Putnam, 1988).

constraints on network membership mean these connections are unlikely to deliver value to managers beyond assistance with the task at hand.

The typical manager in our group was more concerned with sustaining cooperation within the existing network than with building relationships to face nonroutine or unforeseen challenges. But as a manager moves into a leadership role, his or her network must reorient itself externally and toward the future.

Personal Networking

We observed that once aspiring leaders like Alistair awaken to the dangers of an excessively internal focus, they begin to seek kindred spirits outside their organizations. Simultaneously, they become aware of the limitations of their social skills, such as a lack of knowledge about professional domains beyond their own, which makes it difficult for them to find common ground with people outside their usual circles. Through professional associations, alumni groups, clubs, and personal interest communities, managers gain new perspectives that allow them to advance in their careers. This is what we mean by personal networking.

Many of the managers we study question why they should spend precious time on an activity so indirectly related to the work at hand. Why widen one's circle of casual acquaintances when there isn't time even for urgent tasks? The answer is that these contacts provide important referrals, information, and, often, developmental support such as coaching and mentoring. A newly appointed factory director, for example, faced with a turnaround-or-close-down situation that was paralyzing his staff, joined a business organization—and through it met a lawyer who became his counsel in the turnaround. Buoyed by his success, he networked within his company's headquarters in search of someone who had dealt with a similar crisis. Eventually, he found two mentors.

A personal network can also be a safe space for personal development and as such can provide a foundation for strategic networking. The experience of Timothy, a principal in a midsize software company, is a good example. Like his father, Timothy stuttered. When he had the opportunity to prepare for meetings, his stutter was not an issue, but spontaneous encounters inside and outside the company were dreadfully painful. To solve this problem, he began accepting at least two invitations per week to the social gatherings he had assidu-

THE THREE FORMS OF NETWORKING

Managers who think they are adept at networking are often operating only at an operational or personal level. Effective leaders learn to employ networks for strategic purposes.

	Operational	Personal	Strategic
Purpose	Getting work done efficiently; maintaining the capacities and functions required of the group.	Enhancing personal and professional development; providing referrals to useful information and contacts.	Figuring out future priorities and challenges; getting stakeholder support for them.
Location and temporal orientation	Contacts are mostly internal and oriented toward current demands.	Contacts are mostly external and oriented toward current interests and future potential interests.	Contacts are internal and external and oriented toward the future.
Players and recruitment	Key contacts are relatively nondiscretionary; they are prescribed mostly by the task and organizational structure, so it is very clear who is relevant.	Key contacts are mostly discretionary; it is not always clear who is relevant.	Key contacts follow from the strategic context and the organizational environment, but specific membership is discretionary; it is not always clear who is relevant.
Network attributes and key behaviors	Depth: building strong working relationships.	Breadth: reaching out to contacts who can make referrals.	Leverage: creating inside-outside links.

ously ignored before. Before each event, he asked who else had been invited and did background research on the other guests so that he could initiate conversations. The hardest part, he said, was "getting through the door." Once inside, his interest in the conversations helped him forget himself and master his stutter. As his stutter diminished, he also applied himself to networking across his company, whereas previously he had taken refuge in his technical expertise. Like Timothy, several of our emerging leaders successfully used personal networking as a relatively safe way to expose problems and seek insight into solutions—safe, that is, compared with strategic networking, in which the stakes are far higher.

Personal networks are largely external, made up of discretionary links to people with whom we have something in common. As a result, what makes a personal network powerful is its referral potential. According to the famous six degrees of separation principle, our personal contacts are valuable to the extent that they help us reach, in as few connections as possible, the far-off person who has the information we need.

In watching managers struggle to widen their professional relationships in ways that feel both natural and legitimate to them, we repeatedly saw them shift their time and en-ergy from operational to personal networking. For people who have rarely looked outside their organizations, this is an important first step, one that fosters a deeper understanding of themselves and the environments in which they move. Ultimately, however, personal networking alone won't propel managers through the leadership transition. Aspiring leaders may find people who awaken new interests but fail to become comfortable with the power players at the level above them. Or they may achieve new influence within a professional community but fail to harness those ties in the service of organizational goals. That's why managers who know they need to develop their networking skills, and make a real effort to do so, nonetheless may end up feeling like they have wasted their time and energy. As we'll see, personal networking will not help a manager through the leadership transition unless he or she learns how to bring those connections to bear on organizational strategy.

Strategic Networking

When managers begin the delicate transition from functional manager to business leader, they must start to concern themselves with broad strategic issues. Lateral and vertical relationships with other functional and business unit managers—all people outside their im-

---

From Functional Manager to Business Leader: How Companies Can Help

Executives who oversee management development know how to spot critical inflection points: the moments when highly successful people must change their perspective on what is important and, accordingly, how they spend their time. Many organizations still promote people on the basis of their performance in roles whose requirements differ dramatically from those of leadership roles. And many new leaders feel that they are going it alone, without coaching or guidance. By being sensitive to the fact that most strong technical or functional managers lack the capabilities required to build strategic networks that advance their personal and professional goals, human resources and learning professionals can take steps to help in this important area.

For example, Genesis Park, an innovative in-house leadership development program at PricewaterhouseCoopers, focuses explicitly on building networks. The five-month program, during which participants are released from their client responsibilities, includes business case development, strategic projects, team building, change management projects, and in-depth discussions with business leaders from inside and outside the company. The young leaders who participate end up with a strong internal-external nexus of ties to support them as their careers evolve.

Companies that recognize the importance of leadership networking can also do a lot to help people overcome their innate discomfort by creating natural ways for them to extend their networks. When Nissan CEO Carlos Ghosn sought to break down crippling internal barriers at the company, he created cross-functional teams of middle managers from diverse units and charged them with proposing solutions to problems ranging from supply costs to product design. Nissan subsequently institutionalized the teams, not just as a way to solve problems but also to encourage lateral networks. Rather than avoid the extra work, aspiring leaders ask for these assignments.

Most professional development is based on the notion that successful people acquire new role-appropriate skills as they move up the hierarchy. But making the transition from manager to leader requires subtraction as well as addition: To make room for new competencies, managers must rely less on their older, well-honed skills. To do so, they must change their perspective on how to add value and what to contribute. Eventually, they must also transform how they think and who they are. Companies that help their top talent reinvent themselves will better prepare them for a successful leadership transition.

mediate control—become a lifeline for figuring out how their own contributions fit into the big picture. Thus strategic networking plugs the aspiring leader into a set of relationships and information sources that collectively embody the power to achieve personal and organizational goals.

Operating beside players with diverse affiliations, backgrounds, objectives, and incentives requires a manager to formulate business rather than functional objectives, and to work through the coalitions and networks needed to sell ideas and compete for resources. Consider Sophie, a manager who, after rising steadily through the ranks in logistics and distribution, was stupefied to learn that the CEO was considering a radical reorganization of her function that would strip her of some responsibilities. Rewarded to date for incremental annual improvements, she had failed to notice shifting priorities in the wider market and the resulting internal shuffle for resources and power at the higher levels of her company. Although she had built a loyal, high-performing team, she had few relationships outside her group to help her anticipate the new imperatives, let alone give her ideas about how to respond. After she argued that distribution issues were her purview, and failed to be persuasive, she hired consultants to help her prepare a counterproposal. But Sophie's boss simply concluded that she lacked a broad, longer-term business perspective. Frustrated, Sophie contemplated leaving the company. Only after some patient coaching from a senior manager did she understand that she had to get out of her unit and start talking to opinion leaders inside and outside the company to form a sellable plan for the future.

What differentiates a leader from a manager, research tells us, is the ability to figure out where to go and to enlist the people and groups necessary to get there. Recruiting stakeholders, lining up allies and sympathizers, diagnosing the political landscape, and brokering conversations among unconnected parties are all part of a leader's job. As they step up to the leadership transition, some managers accept their growing dependence on others and seek to transform it into mutual influence. Others dismiss such work as "political" and, as a result, undermine their ability to advance their goals.

Several of the participants in our sample chose the latter approach, justifying their choice as a matter of personal values and integrity. In one case, Jody, who managed a department in a large company under what she described as "dysfunctional" leadership, refused even to try to activate her extensive network within the firm when internal adversaries took over key functions of her unit. When we asked her why she didn't seek help from anyone in the organization to stop this coup, she replied that she refused to play "stupid political games....You can only do what you think is the ethical and right thing from your perspective." Stupid or not, those games cost her the respect and support of her direct reports and coworkers, who hesitated to follow someone they perceived as unwilling to defend herself. Eventually she had no choice but to leave.

The key to a good strategic network is leverage: the ability to marshal information, support, and resources from one sector of a network to achieve results in another. Strategic networkers use indirect influence, convincing one person in the network to get someone else, who is not in the network, to take a needed action. Moreover, strategic networkers don't just influence their relational environment; they shape it in their own image by moving and hiring subordinates, changing suppliers and sources of financing, lobbying to place allies in peer positions, and even restructuring their boards to create networks favorable to their business goals. Jody abjured such tactics, but her adversaries did not.

Strategic networking can be difficult for emerging leaders because it absorbs a significant amount of the time and energy that managers usually devote to meeting their many operational demands. This is one reason why many managers drop their strategic networking precisely when they need it most: when their units are in trouble and only outside support can rescue them. The trick is not to hide in the operational network but to develop it into a more strategic one.

One manager we studied, for example, used lateral and functional contacts throughout his firm to resolve tensions with his boss that resulted from substantial differences in style and strategic approaches between the two. Tied down in operational chores at a distant location, the manager had lost contact with headquarters. He resolved the situation by simultaneously obliging his direct reports to take on

As a manager moves into a leadership role, his or her network must reorient itself externally and toward the future.

more of the local management effort and sending messages through his network that would help bring him back into the loop with the boss.

Operational, personal, and strategic networks are not mutually exclusive. One manager we studied used his personal passion, hunting, to meet people from professions as diverse as stonemasonry and household moving. Almost none of these hunting friends had anything to do with his work in the consumer electronics industry, yet they all had to deal with one of his own daily concerns: customer relations. Hearing about their problems and techniques allowed him to view his own from a different perspective and helped him define principles that he could test in his work. Ultimately, what began as a personal network of hunting partners became operationally and strategically valuable to this manager. The key was his ability to build inside-outside links for maximum leverage. But we've seen others who avoided networking, or failed at it, because they let interpersonal chemistry, not strategic needs, determine which relationships they cultivated.

Just Do It

The word "work" is part of networking, and it is not easy work, because it involves reaching outside the borders of a manager's comfort zone. How, then, can managers lessen the pain and increase the gain? The trick is to leverage the elements from each domain of networking into the others—to seek out personal contacts who can be objective, strategic counselors, for example, or to transform colleagues in adjacent functions into a constituency. Above all, many managers will need to change their attitudes about the legitimacy and necessity of networking.

Mind your mind-set. In our ongoing discussions with managers learning to improve their networking skills, we often hear, "That's all well and good, but I already have a day job." Others, like Jody, consider working through networks a way to rely on "whom you know" rather than "what you know"—a hypocritical, even unethical way to get things done. Whatever the reason, when aspiring leaders do not believe that networking is one of the most important requirements of their new jobs, they will not allocate enough time and effort to see it pay off.

The best solution we've seen to this trap is a good role model. Many times, what appears to be unpalatable or unproductive behavior takes on a new light when a person you respect does it well and ethically. For example, Gabriel Chenard, general manager for Europe of a group of consumer product brands, learned from the previous general manager how to take advantage of branch visits to solidify his relationships with employees and customers. Every flight and car trip became a venue for catching up and building relationships with the people who were accompanying him. Watching how much his boss got done on what would otherwise be downtime, Gabriel adopted the practice as a crucial part of his own management style. Networking effectively and ethically, like any other tacit skill, is a matter of judgment and intuition. We learn by observing and getting feedback from those for whom it's second nature.

Work from the outside in. One of the most daunting aspects of strategic networking is that there often seems to be no natural "excuse" for making contact with a more senior person outside one's function or business unit. It's difficult to build a relationship with anyone, let alone a senior executive, without a reason for interacting, like a common task or a shared purpose.

Some successful managers find common ground from the outside in—by, for instance, transposing a personal interest into the strategic domain. Linda Henderson is a good example. An investment banker responsible for a group of media industry clients, she always wondered how to connect to some of her senior colleagues who served other industries. She resolved to make time for an extracurricular passion—the theater—in a way that would enhance her business development activities. Four times a year, her secretary booked a buffet dinner at a downtown hotel and reserved a block of theater tickets. Key clients were invited. Through these events, Linda not only developed her own business but also learned about her clients' companies in a way that generated ideas for other parts of her firm, thus enabling her to engage with colleagues.

Other managers build outside-inside connections by using their functional interests or expertise. For example, communities of practice exist (or can easily be created on the Internet) in almost every area of business from brand management to Six Sigma to global strategy. Savvy managers reach out to kindred spirits outside their organizations to contribute and multiply their knowledge; the information they glean, in more cases than not, becomes the "hook" for making internal connections.

Re-allocate your time. If an aspiring leader has not yet mastered the art of delegation, he or she will find many reasons not to spend time networking. Participating in formal and informal meetings with people in other units takes time away from functional responsibilities and internal team affairs. Between the obvious payoff of a task accomplished and the ambiguous, often delayed rewards of networking, naive managers repeatedly choose the former. The less they practice networking, the less efficient at it they become, and the vicious cycle continues.

Henrik, the production manager and board member we described earlier, for example, did what he needed to do in order to prepare for board meetings but did not associate with fellow board members outside those formal events. As a result, he was frequently surprised when other board members raised issues at the heart of his role. In contrast, effective business leaders spend a lot of time every day gathering the information they need to meet their goals, relying on informal discussions with a lot of people who are not necessarily in charge of an issue or task. They network in order to obtain information continually, not just at formal meetings.

Ask and you shall receive. Many managers equate having a good network with having a large database of contacts, or attending high-profile professional conferences and events. In fact, we've seen people kick off a networking initiative by improving their record keeping or adopting a network management tool. But they falter at the next step—picking up the phone. Instead, they wait until they need something *badly*. The best networkers do exactly the opposite: They take every opportunity to give to, and receive from, the network, whether they need help or not.

A network lives and thrives only when it is used. A good way to begin is to make a simple request or take the initiative to connect two people who would benefit from meeting each other. Doing something—anything—gets the ball rolling and builds confidence that one does, in fact, have something to contribute.

Stick to it. It takes a while to reap the benefits of networking. We have seen many managers resolve to put networking at the top of their agendas, only to be derailed by the first crisis that comes along. One example is Harris Roberts, a regulatory affairs expert who realized he needed a broader network to achieve his goal of becoming a business unit manager. To force himself into what felt like an "unnatural act," Harris volunteered to be the liaison for his business school cohort's alumni network. But six months later, when a major new-drug approval process overwhelmed his calendar, Harris dropped all outside activities. Two years later, he found himself out of touch and still a functional manager. He failed to recognize that by not taking the time to attend industry conferences or compare notes with his peers, he was missing out on the strategic perspective and information that would make him a more attractive candidate for promotion.

Building a leadership network is less a matter of skill than of will. When first efforts do not bring quick rewards, some may simply conclude that networking isn't among their talents. But networking is not a talent; nor does it require a gregarious, extroverted personality. It is a skill, one that takes practice. We have seen over and over again that people who work at networking can learn not only how to do it well but also how to enjoy it. And they tend to be more successful in their careers than those who fail to leverage external ties or insist on defining their jobs narrowly.

Making a successful leadership transition requires a shift from the confines of a clearly defined operational network. Aspiring leaders must learn to build and use strategic networks that cross organizational and functional boundaries, and then link them up in novel and innovative ways. It is a challenge to make the leap from a lifetime of functional contributions and hands-on control to the ambiguous process of building and working through networks. Leaders must find new ways of defining themselves and develop new relationships to anchor and feed their emerging personas. They must also accept that networking is one of the most important requirements of their new leadership roles and continue to allocate enough time and effort to see it pay off.

Reprint R0701C
To order, see the next page
or call 800-988-0886 or 617-783-7500
or go to www.hbrreprints.org

Savvy managers reach out to kindred spirits outside their organizations to contribute and multiply their knowledge; the information they glean, in more cases than not, becomes the "hook" for making internal connections.

How Leaders Create and Use Networks

Further Reading

ARTICLES

Competent Jerks, Lovable Fools, and the Formation of Social Networks
by Tiziana Casciaro and Miguel Sousa Lobo
Harvard Business Review
June 2005
Product no. R0506E

Operational networks pose a dilemma: Do you collaborate on a key project with those colleagues best able to do the job? Or those you like? Many managers opt for likeability over ability. True, good things happen when people who like each other collaborate: Projects flow, and people gladly help each other. But people who like each other typically share values and ways of thinking, so they tend not to generate fresh ideas. They also avoid unpleasant but able colleagues—leaving the expertise of "competent jerks" untapped.

The solution? Support development of positive feelings in critical relationships; for example, by creating cross-departmental project teams to deemphasize functional alliances. Have widely liked individuals serve as evangelists for important change initiatives: people listen to likeable colleagues. And use coaching to burnish competent jerks' social skills.

How to Build Your Network
by Brian Uzzi and Shannon Dunlap
Harvard Business Review
December 2005
Product no. R0512B

The authors provide insights for building your personal network—and transforming it into a more strategic network. A strong personal network helps promote and execute a promising strategy by delivering private information, access to diverse skill sets, and power to the individuals who can implement the plan. But your personal network doesn't just spring into existence at professional association meetings or college reunions. You have to carefully construct it through relatively high-stakes activities that bring you into contact with a diverse group of people. When someone in one cluster of like-minded people within your personal network knows someone else who belongs to a whole different group, this "superconnector" can help you expose your idea to a new world, filled with fresh opportunities for success. The authors explain how to identify superconnectors and diversify your contacts.

Harvard Business Review ⚜

To Order

For *Harvard Business Review* reprints and subscriptions, call 800-988-0886 or 617-783-7500. Go to www.hbrreprints.org

For customized and quantity orders of *Harvard Business Review* article reprints, call 617-783-7626, or e-mail customizations@hbsp.harvard.edu

Harvard Business Review

www.hbrreprints.org

Even the largest and most complex teams can work together effectively if the right conditions are in place.

Eight Ways to Build Collaborative Teams

by Lynda Gratton and Tamara J. Erickson

Included with this full-text *Harvard Business Review* article:

Reprint R0711F

Eight Ways to Build Collaborative Teams

The Idea in Brief

To execute major initiatives in your organization—integrating a newly acquired firm, overhauling an IT system—you need **complex** teams. Such teams' defining characteristics—large, virtual, diverse, and specialized—are crucial for handling daunting projects. Yet these very characteristics can also destroy team members' ability to work together, say Gratton and Erickson. For instance, as team size grows, collaboration diminishes.

To maximize your complex teams' effectiveness, construct a basis for collaboration in your company. Eight practices hinging on relationship building and cultural change can help. For example, create a strong sense of community by sponsoring events and activities that bring people together and help them get to know one another. And use informal mentoring and coaching to encourage employees to view interaction with leaders and colleagues as valuable.

When executives, HR professionals, and team leaders all pitch in to apply these practices, complex teams hit the ground running—the day they're formed.

The Idea in Practice

The authors recommend these practices for encouraging collaboration in complex teams:

WHAT EXECUTIVES CAN DO

- Invest in building and maintaining social relationships throughout your organization.

▶ Example:
Royal Bank of Scotland's CEO commissioned new headquarters built around an indoor atrium and featuring a "Main Street" with shops, picnic spaces, and a leisure club. The design encourages employees to rub shoulders daily, which fuels collaboration in RBS's complex teams.

- Model collaborative behavior.

▶ Example:
At Standard Chartered Bank, top executives frequently fill in for one another, whether leading regional celebrations, representing SCB at key external events, or initiating internal dialogues with employees. They make their collaborative behavior visible through extensive travel and photos of leaders from varied sites working together.

- Use coaching to reinforce a collaborative culture.

▶ Example:
At Nokia, each new hire's manager lists everyone in the organization the newcomer should meet, suggests topics he or she should discuss with each person on the list, and explains why establishing each of these relationships is important.

WHAT HR CAN DO

- Train employees in the specific skills required for collaboration: appreciating others, engaging in purposeful conversation, productively and creatively resolving conflicts, and managing programs.

- Support a sense of community by sponsoring events and activities such as networking groups, cooking weekends, or tennis coaching. Spontaneous, unannounced activities can further foster community spirit.

▶ Example:
Marriott has recognized the anniversary of the company's first hotel opening by rolling back the cafeteria to the 1950s and sponsoring a team twist dance contest.

WHAT TEAM LEADERS CAN DO

- Ensure that at least 20%–40% of a new team's members already know one another.

▶ Example:
When Nokia needs to transfer skills across business functions or units, it moves entire small teams intact instead of reshuffling individual people into new positions.

- Change your leadership style as your team develops. At early stages in the project, be task-oriented: articulate the team's goal and accountabilities. As inevitable conflicts start emerging, switch to relationship building.

- Assign distinct roles so team members can do their work independently. They'll spend less time negotiating responsibilities or protecting turf. But leave the *path* to achieving the team's goal somewhat ambiguous. Lacking well-defined tasks, members are more likely to invest time and energy collaborating.

Even the largest and most complex teams can work together effectively if the right conditions are in place.

Eight Ways to Build Collaborative Teams

by Lynda Gratton and Tamara J. Erickson

When tackling a major initiative like an acquisition or an overhaul of IT systems, companies rely on large, diverse teams of highly educated specialists to get the job done. These teams often are convened quickly to meet an urgent need and work together virtually, collaborating online and sometimes over long distances.

Appointing such a team is frequently the only way to assemble the knowledge and breadth required to pull off many of the complex tasks businesses face today. When the BBC covers the World Cup or the Olympics, for instance, it gathers a large team of researchers, writers, producers, cameramen, and technicians, many of whom have not met before the project. These specialists work together under the high pressure of a "no retake" environment, with just one chance to record the action. Similarly, when the central IT team at Marriott sets out to develop sophisticated systems to enhance guest experiences, it has to collaborate closely with independent hotel owners, customer-experience experts, global brand managers, and regional heads, each with his or her own agenda and needs.

Our recent research into team behavior at 15 multinational companies, however, reveals an interesting paradox: Although teams that are large, virtual, diverse, and composed of highly educated specialists are increasingly crucial with challenging projects, those same four characteristics make it hard for teams to get anything done. To put it another way, the qualities required for success are the same qualities that undermine success. Members of complex teams are less likely—*absent other influences*—to share knowledge freely, to learn from one another, to shift workloads flexibly to break up unexpected bottlenecks, to help one another complete jobs and meet deadlines, and to share resources—in other words, to collaborate. They are less likely to say that they "sink or swim" together, want one another to succeed, or view their goals as compatible.

Consider the issue of size. Teams have grown considerably over the past ten years. New technologies help companies extend participation on a project to an ever greater number of people, allowing firms to tap into a wide body of knowledge and expertise. A decade or so ago, the common view was that true teams rarely had more than 20 members. Today, according to our research, many complex tasks involve teams of 100 or more. However, as the size of a team increases beyond 20 members, the tendency to collaborate naturally decreases, we have found. Under the right conditions, large teams can achieve high levels of cooperation, but creating those conditions requires thoughtful, and sometimes significant, investments in the capacity for collaboration across the organization.

Working together virtually has a similar impact on teams. The majority of those we studied had members spread among multiple locations—in several cases, in as many as 13 sites around the globe. But as teams became more virtual, we saw, cooperation also declined, unless the company had taken measures to establish a collaborative culture.

As for diversity, the challenging tasks facing businesses today almost always require the input and expertise of people with disparate views and backgrounds to create cross-fertilization that sparks insight and innovation. But diversity also creates problems. Our research shows that team members collaborate more easily and naturally if they perceive themselves as being alike. The differences that inhibit collaboration include not only nationality but also age, educational level, and even tenure. Greater diversity also often means that team members are working with people that they know only superficially or have never met before—colleagues drawn from other divisions of the company, perhaps, or even from outside it. We have found that the higher the proportion of strangers on the team and the greater the diversity of background and experience, the less likely team members are to share knowledge or exhibit other collaborative behaviors.

In the same way, the higher the educational level of the team members is, the more challenging collaboration appears to be for them. We found that the greater the proportion of experts a team had, the more likely it was to disintegrate into nonproductive conflict or stalemate.

So how can executives strengthen an organization's ability to perform complex collaborative tasks—to maximize the effectiveness of large, diverse teams, while minimizing the disadvantages posed by their structure and composition?

To answer that question we looked carefully at 55 large teams and identified those that demonstrated high levels of collaborative behavior despite their complexity. Put differently, they succeeded both because of and despite their composition. Using a range of statistical analyses, we considered how more than 100 factors, such as the design of the task and the company culture, might contribute to collaboration, manifested, for example, in a willingness to share knowledge and workloads. Out of the 100-plus factors, we were able to isolate eight practices that correlated with success—that is, that appeared to help teams overcome substantially the difficulties that were posed by size, long-distance communication, diversity, and specialization. We then interviewed the teams that were very strong in these practices, to find out how they did it. In this article we'll walk through the practices. They fall into four general categories—executive support, HR practices, the strength of the team leader, and the structure of the team itself.

Executive Support

At the most basic level, a team's success or failure at collaborating reflects the philosophy of top executives in the organization. Teams do well when executives invest in supporting social relationships, demonstrate collaborative behavior themselves, and create what we call a "gift culture"—one in which employees experience interactions with leaders and colleagues as something valuable and generously offered, a gift.

Investing in signature relationship practices. When we looked at complex collaborative teams that were performing in a productive and innovative manner, we found that in every case the company's top executives had invested significantly in building and maintaining social relationships throughout the organization. However, the way they did that varied widely. The most collaborative companies had what we call "signature" practices—practices that were memorable, difficult for others to replicate, and particularly well suited to their own business environment.

For example, when Royal Bank of Scotland's CEO, Fred Goodwin, invested £350 million to

Lynda Gratton (lgratton@london.edu) is a professor of management practice at London Business School and a senior fellow at the Advanced Institute of Management. She is the author of *Hot Spots: Why Some Teams, Workplaces, and Organizations Buzz with Energy—and Others Don't* (Berrett-Koehler, 2007). **Tamara J. Erickson** (tjerickson@concoursgroup.com) is the president of the Concours Institute, the research and education arm of BSG Alliance. She is based in Boston and is a coauthor of several articles for HBR, including the McKinsey Award winner "It's Time to Retire Retirement" (March 2004).

open a new headquarters building outside Edinburgh in 2005, one of his goals was to foster productive collaboration among employees. Built around an indoor atrium, the new structure allows more than 3,000 people from the firm to rub shoulders daily.

The headquarters is designed to improve communication, increase the exchange of ideas, and create a sense of community among employees. Many of the offices have an open layout and look over the atrium—a vast transparent space. The campus is set up like a small town, with retail shops, restaurants, jogging tracks and cycling trails, spaces for picnics and barbecues—even a leisure club complete with swimming pool, gym, dance studios, tennis courts, and football pitches. The idea is that with a private "Main Street" running through the headquarters, employees will remain on the campus throughout the day—and be out of their offices mingling with colleagues for at least a portion of it.

To ensure that non-headquarters staff members feel they are a part of the action, Good-

win also commissioned an adjoining business school, where employees from other locations meet and learn. The visitors are encouraged to spend time on the headquarters campus and at forums designed to give employees opportunities to build relationships.

Indeed, the RBS teams we studied had very strong social relationships, a solid basis for collaborative activity that allowed them to accomplish tasks quickly. Take the Group Business Improvement (GBI) teams, which work on 30-, 60-, or 90-day projects ranging from back-office fixes to IT updates and are made up of people from across RBS's many businesses, including insurance, retail banking, and private banking in Europe and the United States. When RBS bought NatWest and migrated the new acquisition's technology platform to RBS's, the speed and success of the GBI teams confounded many market analysts.

BP has made another sort of signature investment. Because its employees are located all over the world, with relatively few at headquarters, the company aims to build social

The Research

Our work is based on a major research initiative conducted jointly by the Concours Institute (a member of BSG Alliance) and the Cooperative Research Project of London Business School, with funding from the Advanced Institute for Management and 15 corporate sponsors. The initiative was created as a way to explore the practicalities of collaborative work in contemporary organizations.

We sent surveys to 2,420 people, including members of 55 teams. A total of 1,543 people replied, a response rate of 64%. Separate surveys were administered to group members, to group leaders, to the executives who evaluated teams, and to HR leaders at the companies involved. The tasks performed by the teams included new-product development, process reengineering, and identifying new solutions to business problems. The companies involved included four telecommunication companies, seven financial services or consulting firms, two media companies, a hospitality firm, and one oil company. The size of the teams ranged from four to 183 people, with an average of 44.

Our objective was to study the levers that executives could pull to improve team performance and innovation in collaborative tasks. We examined scores of possible factors, including the following:

The general culture of the company. We designed a wide range of survey questions to measure the extent to which the firm had a cooperative culture and to uncover employees' attitudes toward knowledge sharing.

Human resources practices and processes. We studied the way staffing took place and the process by which people were promoted. We examined the extent and type of training, how reward systems were configured, and the extent to which mentoring and coaching took place.

Socialization and network-building practices. We looked at how often people within the team participated in informal socialization, and the type of interaction that was most common. We also asked numerous questions about the extent to which team members were active in informal communities.

The design of the task. We asked team members and team leaders about the task

itself. Our interest here was in how they perceived the purpose of the task, how complex it was, the extent to which the task required members of the team to be interdependent, and the extent to which the task required them to engage in boundary-spanning activities with people outside the team.

The leadership of the team. We studied the perceptions team members had of their leaders' style and how the leaders described their own style. In particular, we were interested in the extent to which the leaders practiced relationship-oriented and task-oriented skills and set cooperative or competitive goals.

The behavior of the senior executives. We asked team members and team leaders about their perceptions of the senior executives of their business unit. We focused in particular on whether team members described them as cooperative or competitive.

In total we considered more than 100 factors. Using a range of statistical analyses, we were able to identify eight that correlated with the successful performance of teams handling complex collaborative tasks. (See the sidebar "Eight Factors That Lead to Success.")

networks by moving employees across functions, businesses, and countries as part of their career development. When BP integrates an acquisition (it has grown by buying numerous smaller oil companies), the leadership development committee deliberately rotates employees from the acquired firm through positions across the corporation. Though the easier and cheaper call would be to leave the executives in their own units—where, after all, they know the business—BP instead trains them to take on new roles. As a consequence any senior team today is likely to be made up of people from multiple heritages. Changing roles frequently—it would not be uncommon for a senior leader at BP to have worked in four businesses and three geographic locations over the past decade—forces executives to become very good at meeting new people and building relationships with them.

Collaboration Conundrums

Four traits that are crucial to teams—but also undermine them

Large Size
Whereas a decade ago, teams rarely had more than 20 members, our findings show that their size has increased significantly, no doubt because of new technologies. Large teams are often formed to ensure the involvement of a wide stakeholder group, the coordination of a diverse set of activities, and the harnessing of multiple skills. As a consequence, many inevitably involve 100 people or more. However, our research shows that as the size of the team increases beyond 20 members, the level of natural cooperation among members of the team decreases.

Virtual Participation
Today most complex collaborative teams have members who are working at a distance from one another. Again, the logic is that the assigned tasks require the insights and knowledge of people from many locations. Team members may be working in offices in the same city or strung across the world. Only 40% of the

teams in our sample had members all in one place. Our research shows that as teams become more virtual, collaboration declines.

Diversity
Often the challenging tasks facing today's businesses require the rapid assembly of people from multiple backgrounds and perspectives, many of whom have rarely, if ever, met. Their diverse knowledge and views can spark insight and innovation. However, our research shows that the higher the proportion of people who don't know anyone else on the team and the greater the diversity, the less likely the team members are to share knowledge.

High Education Levels
Complex collaborative teams often generate huge value by drawing on a variety of deeply specialized skills and knowledge to devise new solutions. Again, however, our research shows that the greater the proportion of highly educated specialists on a team, the more likely the team is to disintegrate into unproductive conflicts.

Modeling collaborative behavior. In companies with many thousands of employees, relatively few have the opportunity to observe the behavior of the senior team on a day-to-day basis. Nonetheless, we found that the perceived behavior of senior executives plays a significant role in determining how cooperative teams are prepared to be.

Executives at Standard Chartered Bank are exceptionally good role models when it comes to cooperation, a strength that many attribute to the firm's global trading heritage. The Chartered Bank received its remit from Queen Victoria in 1853. The bank's traditional business was in cotton from Bombay (now Mumbai), indigo and tea from Calcutta, rice from Burma, sugar from Java, tobacco from Sumatra, hemp from Manila, and silk from Yokohama. The Standard Bank was founded in the Cape Province of South Africa in 1863 and was prominent in financing the development of the diamond fields and later gold mines. Standard Chartered was formed in 1969 through a merger of the two banks, and today the firm has 57 operating groups in 57 countries, with no home market.

It's widely accepted at Standard Chartered that members of the general management committee will frequently serve as substitutes for one another. The executives all know and understand the entire business and can fill in for each other easily on almost any task, whether it's leading a regional celebration, representing the company at a key external event, or kicking off an internal dialogue with employees.

While the behavior of the executive team is crucial to supporting a culture of collaboration, the challenge is to make executives' behavior visible. At Standard Chartered the senior team travels extensively; the norm is to travel even for relatively brief meetings. This investment in face-to-face interaction creates many opportunities for people across the company to see the top executives in action. Internal communication is frequent and open, and, maybe most telling, every site around the world is filled with photos of groups of executives—country and functional leaders—working together.

The senior team's collaborative nature trickles down throughout the organization. Employees quickly learn that the best way to get things done is through informal networks.

For example, when a major program was recently launched to introduce a new customer-facing technology, the team responsible had an almost uncanny ability to understand who the key stakeholders at each branch bank were and how best to approach them. The team members' first-name acquaintance with people across the company brought a sense of dynamism to their interactions.

Creating a "gift culture." A third important role for executives is to ensure that mentoring and coaching become embedded in their own routine behavior—and throughout the company. We looked at both formal mentoring processes, with clear roles and responsibilities, and less formal processes, where mentoring was integrated into everyday activities. It turned out that while both types were important, the latter was more likely to increase collaborative behavior. Daily coaching helps establish a cooperative "gift culture" in place of a more transactional "tit-for-tat culture."

At Nokia informal mentoring begins as soon as someone steps into a new job. Typically, within a few days, the employee's manager will sit down and list all the people in the organization, no matter in what location, it would be useful for the employee to meet. This is a deeply ingrained cultural norm, which probably originated when Nokia was a smaller and simpler organization. The manager sits with the newcomer, just as her manager sat with her when she joined, and reviews what topics the newcomer should discuss with each person on the list and why establishing a relationship with him or her is important. It is then standard for the newcomer to actively set up meetings with the people on the list, even when it means traveling to other locations. The gift of time—in the form of hours spent on coaching and building networks—is seen as crucial to the collaborative culture at Nokia.

Focused HR Practices

So what about human resources? Is collaboration solely in the hands of the executive team? In our study we looked at the impact of a wide variety of HR practices, including selection, performance management, promotion, rewards, and training, as well as formally sponsored coaching and mentoring programs.

We found some surprises: for example, that the type of reward system—whether based on team or individual achievement, or tied explicitly to collaborative behavior or not—had no discernible effect on complex teams' productivity and innovation. Although most formal HR programs appeared to have limited impact, we found that two practices did improve team performance: training in skills related to collaborative behavior, and support for informal community building. Where collaboration was strong, the HR team had typically made a significant investment in one or both of those practices—often in ways that uniquely represented the company's culture and business strategy.

Eight Factors That Lead to Success

1. Investing in signature relationship practices. Executives can encourage collaborative behavior by making highly visible investments—in facilities with open floor plans to foster communication, for example—that demonstrate their commitment to collaboration.

2. Modeling collaborative behavior. At companies where the senior executives demonstrate highly collaborative behavior themselves, teams collaborate well.

3. Creating a "gift culture." Mentoring and coaching—especially on an informal basis—help people build the networks they need to work across corporate boundaries.

4. Ensuring the requisite skills. Human resources departments that teach employees how to build relationships, communicate well, and resolve conflicts creatively can have a major impact on team collaboration.

5. Supporting a strong sense of community. When people feel a sense of community, they are more comfortable reaching out to others and more likely to share knowledge.

6. Assigning team leaders that are both task- and relationship-oriented. The debate has traditionally focused on whether a task or a relationship orientation creates better leadership, but in fact both are key to successfully leading a team. Typically, leaning more heavily on a task orientation at the outset of a project and shifting toward a relationship orientation once the work is in full swing works best.

7. Building on heritage relationships. When too many team members are strangers, people may be reluctant to share knowledge. The best practice is to put at least a few people who know one another on the team.

8. Understanding role clarity and task ambiguity. Cooperation increases when the roles of individual team members are sharply defined yet the team is given latitude on how to achieve the task.

Ensuring the requisite skills. Many of the factors that support collaboration relate to what we call the "container" of collaboration—the underlying culture and habits of the company or team. However, we found that some teams had a collaborative culture but were not skilled in the practice of collaboration itself. They were encouraged to cooperate, they wanted to cooperate, but they didn't know how to work together very well in teams.

Our study showed that a number of skills were crucial: appreciating others, being able to engage in purposeful conversations, productively and creatively resolving conflicts, and program management. By training employees in those areas, a company's human resources or corporate learning department can make an important difference in team performance.

In the research, PricewaterhouseCoopers emerged as having one of the strongest capabilities in productive collaboration. With responsibility for developing 140,000 employees in nearly 150 countries, PwC's training includes modules that address teamwork, emotional intelligence, networking, holding difficult conversations, coaching, corporate social responsibility, and communicating the firm's strategy and shared values. PwC also teaches employees how to influence others effectively and build healthy partnerships.

A number of other successful teams in our sample came from organizations that had a commitment to teaching employees relationship skills. Lehman Brothers' flagship program for its client-facing staff, for instance, is its training in selling and relationship management. The program is not about sales techniques but, rather, focuses on how Lehman values its clients and makes sure that every client has access to all the resources the firm has to offer. It is essentially a course on strategies for building collaborative partnerships with customers, emphasizing the importance of trust-based personal relationships.

Supporting a sense of community. While a communal spirit can develop spontaneously, we discovered that HR can also play a critical role in cultivating it, by sponsoring group events and activities such as women's networks, cooking weekends, and tennis coaching, or creating policies and practices that encourage them.

At ABN Amro we studied effective change-management teams within the company's enterprise services function. These informal groups were responsible for projects associated with the implementation of new technology throughout the bank; one team, for instance, was charged with expanding online banking services. To succeed, the teams needed the involvement and expertise of different parts of the organization.

The ABN Amro teams rated the company's support for informal communities very positively. The firm makes the technology needed for long-distance collaboration readily available to groups of individuals with shared interests—for instance, in specific technologies or markets—who hold frequent web conferences and communicate actively online. The company also encourages employees that travel to a new location to arrange meetings with as many people as possible. As projects are completed, working groups disband but employees maintain networks of connections. These practices serve to build a strong community over time—one that sets the stage for success with future projects.

Committed investment in informal networks is also a central plank of the HR strategy at Marriott. Despite its size and global reach, Marriott remains a family business, and the chairman, Bill Marriott, makes a point of communicating that idea regularly to employees. He still tells stories of counting sticky nickels at night as a child—proceeds from the root-beer stand founded in downtown Washington, DC, by his mother and father.

How Complex Is the Collaborative Task?

Not all highly collaborative tasks are complex. In assembling and managing a team, consider the project you need to assign and whether the following statements apply:

__ The task is unlikely to be accomplished successfully using only the skills within the team.

__ The task must be addressed by a new group formed specifically for this purpose.

__ The task requires collective input from highly specialized individuals.

__ The task requires collective input and agreement from more than 20 people.

__ The members of the team working on the task are in more than two locations.

__ The success of the task is highly dependent on understanding preferences or needs of individuals outside the group.

__ The outcome of the task will be influenced by events that are highly uncertain and difficult to predict.

__ The task must be completed under extreme time pressure.

If more than two of these statements are true, the task requires complex collaboration.

Many of the firm's HR investments reinforce a friendly, family-like culture. Almost every communication reflects an element of staff appreciation. A range of "pop-up" events—spontaneous activities—create a sense of fun and community. For example, the cafeteria might roll back to the 1950s, hold a twist dance contest, and in doing so, recognize the anniversary of the company's first hotel opening. Bill Marriott's birthday might be celebrated with parties throughout the company, serving as an occasion to emphasize the firm's culture and values. The chairman recently began his own blog, which is popular with employees, in which he discusses everything from Marriott's efforts to become greener, to his favorite family vacation spots—themes intended to reinforce the idea that the company is a community.

The Right Team Leaders

In the groups that had high levels of collaborative behavior, the team leaders clearly made a significant difference. The question in our minds was how they actually achieved this. The answer, we saw, lay in their flexibility as managers.

Assigning leaders who are both task- and relationship-oriented. There has been much debate among both academics and senior managers about the most appropriate style for leading teams. Some people have suggested that relationship-oriented leadership is most appropriate in complex teams, since people are more likely to share knowledge in an environment of trust and goodwill. Others have argued that a task orientation—the ability to make objectives clear, to create a shared awareness of the dimensions of the task, and to provide monitoring and feedback—is most important.

In the 55 teams we studied, we found that the truth lay somewhere in between. The most productive, innovative teams were typically led by people who were *both* task- and relationship-oriented. What's more, these leaders changed their style during the project. Specifically, at the early stages they exhibited task-oriented leadership: They made the goal clear, engaged in debates about commitments, and clarified the responsibilities of individual team members. However, at a certain point in the development of the project they switched to a relationship orientation.

This shift often took place once team members had nailed down the goals and their accountabilities and when the initial tensions around sharing knowledge had begun to emerge. An emphasis throughout a project on one style at the expense of the other inevitably hindered the long-term performance of the team, we found.

Producing ambidextrous team leaders—those with both relationship and task skills—is a core goal of team-leadership development at Marriott. The company's performance-review process emphasizes growth in both kinds of skills. As evidence of their relationship skills, managers are asked to describe their peer network and cite examples of specific ways that network helped them succeed. They also must provide examples of how they've used relationship building to get things done. The development plans that follow these conversations explicitly map out how the managers can improve specific elements of their social relationships and networks. Such a plan might include, for instance, having lunch regularly with people from a particular community of interest.

To improve their task leadership, many people in the teams at Marriott participated in project-management certification programs, taking refresher courses to maintain their skills over time. Evidence of both kinds of capabilities becomes a significant criterion on which people are selected for key leadership roles at the company.

Team Formation and Structure

The final set of lessons for developing and managing complex teams has to do with the makeup and structure of the teams themselves.

Building on heritage relationships. Given how important trust is to successful collaboration, forming teams that capitalize on preexisting, or "heritage," relationships, increases the chances of a project's success. Our research shows that new teams, particularly those with a high proportion of members who were strangers at the time of formation, find it more difficult to collaborate than those with established relationships.

Newly formed teams are forced to invest significant time and effort in building trusting relationships. However, when some team members already know and trust one an-

The most productive, innovative teams were led by people who were both task- and relationship-oriented. What's more, these leaders changed their style during the project.

other, they can become nodes, which over time evolve into networks. Looking closely at our data, we discovered that when 20% to 40% of the team members were already well connected to one another, the team had strong collaboration right from the start.

It helps, of course, if the company leadership has taken other measures to cultivate networks that cross boundaries. The orientation process at Nokia ensures that a large number of people on any team know one another, increasing the odds that even in a company of more than 100,000 people, someone on a companywide team knows someone else and can make introductions.

Nokia has also developed an organizational architecture designed to make good use of heritage relationships. When it needs to transfer skills across business functions or units, Nokia moves entire small teams intact instead of reshuffling individual people into new positions. If, for example, the company needs to bring together a group of market and technology experts to address a new customer need, the group formed would be composed of small pods of colleagues from each area. This ensures that key heritage relationships continue to strengthen over time, even as the organization redirects its resources to meet market needs. Because the entire company has one common platform for logistics, HR, finance, and other transactions, teams can switch in and out of businesses and geographies without learning new systems.

One important caveat about heritage relationships: If not skillfully managed, too many of them can actually disrupt collaboration. When a significant number of people within the team know one another, they tend to form strong subgroups—whether by function, geography, or anything else they have in common. When that happens, the probability of conflict among the subgroups, which we call fault lines, increases.

Understanding role clarity and task ambiguity. Which is more important to promoting collaboration: a clearly defined approach toward achieving the goal, or clearly specified roles for individual team members? The common assumption is that carefully spelling out the approach is essential, but leaving the roles of individuals within the team vague will encourage people to share ideas and contribute in multiple dimensions.

Our research shows that the opposite is true: Collaboration improves when the roles of individual team members are clearly defined and well understood—when individuals feel that they can do a significant portion of their work independently. Without such clarity, team members are likely to waste too much energy negotiating roles or protecting turf, rather than focus on the task. In addition, team members are more likely to want to collaborate if the path to achieving the team's goal is left somewhat ambiguous. If a team perceives the task as one that requires creativity, where the approach is not yet well known or predefined, its members are more likely to invest time and energy in collaboration.

At the BBC we studied the teams responsible for the radio and television broadcasts of the 2006 Proms (a two-month-long musical celebration), the team that televised the 2006 World Cup, and a team responsible for daytime television news. These teams were large—133 people worked on the Proms, 66 on the World Cup, and 72 on the news—and included members with a wide range of skills and from many disciplines. One would imagine, therefore, that there was a strong possibility of confusion among team members.

To the contrary, we found that the BBC's teams scored among the highest in our sample with regard to the clarity with which members viewed their own roles and the roles of others. Every team was composed of specialists who had deep expertise in their given function, and each person had a clearly defined role. There was little overlap between the responsibilities of the sound technician and the camera operator, and so on. Yet the tasks the BBC teams tackle are, by their very nature, uncertain, particularly when they involve breaking news. The trick the BBC has pulled off has been to clarify team members' individual roles with so much precision that it keeps friction to a minimum.

The successful teams we studied at Reuters worked out of far-flung locations, and often the team members didn't speak a common language. (The primary languages were Russian, Chinese, Thai, and English.) These teams, largely composed of software programmers, were responsible for the rapid development of highly complex technical software and network products. Many of the programmers sat at their desks for 12 hours straight developing code, speaking with no one. Ironically, these teams judged cooperative behavior to be high among their members. That may be because each individual was given autonomy over one discrete piece of the project. The rapid pace and demanding project timelines encouraged individual members to work independently to get the job done, but each person's work had to be shaped with an eye toward the overall team goal.

• • •

Strengthening your organization's capacity for collaboration requires a combination of long-term investments—in building relationships and trust, in developing a culture in which senior leaders are role models of cooperation—and smart near-term decisions about the ways teams are formed, roles are defined, and challenges and tasks are articulated. Practices and structures that may have worked well with simple teams of people who were all in one lo-cation and knew one another are likely to lead to failure when teams grow more complex.

Most of the factors that impede collabora-tion today would have impeded collaboration at any time in history. Yesterday's teams, how-ever, didn't require the same amount of mem-bers, diversity, long-distance cooperation, or expertise that teams now need to solve global business challenges. So the models for teams need to be realigned with the demands of the current business environment. Through care-ful attention to the factors we've described in this article, companies can assemble the breadth of expertise needed to solve complex business problems—without inducing the destructive behaviors that can accompany it.

Reprint R0711F
To order, see the next page
or call 800-988-0886 or 617-783-7500
or go to www.hbrreprints.org

Eight Ways to Build Collaborative Teams

Further Reading

ARTICLES

Can Absence Make a Team Grow Stronger?
by Ann Majchrzak, Arvind Malhotra, Jeffrey Stamps, and Jessica Lipnack
Harvard Business Review
May 2004
Product no. R0405J

The authors focus on the virtual nature of complex teams, arguing that companies don't need to bring far-flung team members together to get their best work. When people collaborate virtually, they feel freer to contribute outside their areas of expertise. And because they don't have to wait for meetings to make decisions, their projects advance faster. But to reap these advantages, team leaders must manage work processes and social dynamics shrewdly. For example, rather than depend on videoconferencing or e-mail, which can be unwieldy or exclusionary, use online team rooms, where everyone can easily see projects' status, discuss the work, and be reminded of decisions and commitments. Hash out differences in teleconferences, which also help foster group identity and solidarity.

Boosting Your Team's Emotional Intelligence—for Maximum Performance
by Daniel Goleman, Vanessa Urch Druskat, Steven B. Wolff, Jon R. Katzenbach, and Douglas K. Smith
HBR Article Collection
March 2001
Product no. 617X

Emotional intelligence is a key collaboration skill. This collection explains how teams can perform more effectively by sharpening their EI. In "What Makes a Leader?" Daniel Goleman defines the five competencies of EI for individuals, which include knowledge of one's weaknesses and ability to control one's impulses. In "Building the Emotional Intelligence of Groups," Vanessa Urch Druskat and Steven Wolff take EI to the team level, outlining norms groups need to strengthen their emotional intelligence. Norms include letting the group express emotions and handling conflict constructively. In "The Discipline of Teams," Jon Katzenbach and Douglas Smith address another building block of team EI: mutual accountability based on collective discipline. A disciplined team has several defining characteristics, including a common purpose and specific performance goals.

Harvard Business Review

To Order

For *Harvard Business Review* reprints and subscriptions, call 800-988-0886 or 617-783-7500. Go to www.hbrreprints.org

For customized and quantity orders of *Harvard Business Review* article reprints, call 617-783-7626, or e-mail customizations@hbsp.harvard.edu

Harvard Business Review ⬥

www.hbr.org

You're ready to chuck it all and start afresh. Just make sure you don't listen to the usual advice about changing careers.

How to Stay Stuck in the Wrong Career

by Herminia Ibarra

Included with this full-text *Harvard Business Review* article:

Reprint R0212B

How to Stay Stuck in the Wrong Career

The Idea in Brief

Are you one of the growing number of people struggling to make mid-career changes? Searching for ten easy steps to professional reinvention? Or awaiting flashes of insight—while opportunities pass you by?

Would you be willing to jettison all you've heard about career transition and follow a crooked path—rather than the straight and narrow one that's gotten you nowhere?

If so, consider the counterintuitive approach described in this article. It'll have you *doing* instead of infinitely planning. Taking *action* instead of endless self-assessment tests. You'll reinvent your **working identity**— your sense of who you are as a professional— by experimenting with who you *could* be.

The Idea in Practice

SOUNDS REASONABLE, BUT...

Consider the traditional "plan and implement" approach to career change: Assess your interests, skills, and experience; identify appropriate jobs; consult friends, colleagues, career counselors; take the plunge.

This all *sounds* reasonable—but it actually fosters stagnation. You get mired in introspection while searching for your "one true self "a futile quest, since individuals have many possible selves. Your ideal won't necessarily find a match in the real world. Worse, this method encourages making a big change all at once—which can land you in the wrong job.

SOUNDS CRAZY, BUT...

Now consider the "test and learn" method: You put *several* working identities into practice, refining them until they're sufficiently grounded in experience to inspire more decisive steps. You make your possible *future* working identities vivid, tangible, and compelling—countering the tendency to grab familiar work when the unknown becomes too scary.

Reinventing your working identity takes several years—and may land you in surprising places. But that doesn't mean the process must be random. These tactics provide a method to the seeming madness:

- **Craft experiments.** Play with new professional roles on a limited but tangible scale, without compromising your current job. Try freelance assignments or pro bono work. Moonlight. Use sabbaticals or extended vacations to explore new directions.

  ▶ Example:
  A former investment banker dabbled in wine tours and scuba diving businesses before determining that such work wouldn't hold his interest long-term. Realizing a "more normal" career path would better serve his emotional and financial needs, he

is now a internal venture capitalist for a media company.

- **Shift connections.** Strangers can best help you see who you're becoming, providing fresh ideas uncolored by your previous identity. Make new connections by working for people you've long admired and can learn from. Find people—perhaps through alumni and company networks—who can help you grow into your possible new selves.

- **Make sense.** Infuse events with special meaning. Weave them into a story about who you're becoming. Relate that story publicly. You'll clarify your intentions, stay motivated, and inspire others' support.

  ▶ Example:
  An investment banker considering fiction writing visited an astrologer, who noted that forces pulling him in opposing directions (stability versus creative expression) were irreconcilable. He told everyone this story and wrote about it in his local newspaper. The more he communicated it, the more the incident made sense—and the more friends and family supported his writing ambitions.

You're ready to chuck it all and start afresh. Just make sure you don't listen to the usual advice about changing careers.

How to Stay Stuck in the Wrong Career

by Herminia Ibarra

Everyone knows a story about a smart and talented businessperson who has lost his or her passion for work, who no longer looks forward to going to the office yet remains stuck without a visible way out. Most everyone knows a story, too, about a person who ditched a 20-year career to pursue something completely different—the lawyer who gave it all up to become a writer or the auditor who quit her accounting firm to start her own toy company—and is the happier for it.

"Am I doing what is right for me, or should I change direction?" is one of the most pressing questions in the mid-career professional's mind today. The numbers of people making major career changes, not to mention those just thinking about it, have risen significantly over the last decade and continue to grow. But the difference between the person who yearns for change yet stays put and the person who takes the leap to find renewed fulfillment at midcareer is not what you might expect. Consider the following examples:

Susan Fontaine made a clean break with her unfulfilling past as partner and head of the strategy practice at a top consulting firm. But the former management consultant—her name, like the names of the other people I studied, has been changed for this article—had not yet had the time to figure out a future direction. When a close client offered her the top strategy job at a *Financial Times* 100 firm, she took it. She was ready for change, and the opportunity was too good to pass up. To her dismay, this position—though perfect according to what she calls "the relentless logic of a post-MBA CV"—was no different from her old job in all the aspects she had been seeking to change. Two weeks into the new role, she realized she had made a terrible mistake.

After a four-week executive education program at a top business school, Harris Roberts, a regulatory affairs director at a major health care firm, was ready for change. He wanted bottom-line responsibility, and he itched to put into practice some of the cutting-edge ideas he had learned in the program. His long-time mentor, the company's CEO, had promised, "When you come back, we'll give you a business unit." But upon Harris's return, a complicated new product introduction delayed the long-awaited transition. He was needed in his old role, so he was asked to postpone his dream. As always, Harris put the company first. But he was disappointed; there was no challenge anymore. Resigned to waiting it out, he created for himself a "network of mentors," senior members of the firm whom he enlisted to guide his development and help him try to land the coveted general management role. Eighteen months later, he was still doing essentially the same job.

A milestone birthday, upheaval in his personal life, and a negative performance evaluation—the first of his career—combined to make a "snapping point" for Gary McCarthy. After business school, the former investment banker and consultant had taken a job at a blue-chip firm by default, biding his time until he found his "true passion." Now, he decided, it was time to make a proactive career choice. Determined to get it right, Gary did all the correct things. He started with a career psychologist who gave him a battery of tests to help him figure out his work interests and values. He talked to headhunters, friends, and family and read bestselling books on career change. By his own account, none of the advice was very useful. He researched possible industries and companies. He made two lists: completely different professions involving things he was passionate about and variations on what he was already doing. A year later, a viable alternative had yet to materialize.

When I consider the experiences of these people and dozens of others I have studied over the past few years, there can be no doubt: Despite the rhetoric, a true change of direction is very hard to swing. This isn't because managers or professionals are typically unwilling to change; on the contrary, many make serious attempts to reinvent themselves, devoting large amounts of time and energy to the process at great professional and personal risk. But despite heroic efforts, they remain stuck in the wrong careers, not living up to their potential and sacrificing professional fulfillment.

Many academics and career counselors observe this inertia and conclude that the problem lies in basic human motives: We fear change, lack readiness, are unwilling to make sacrifices, sabotage ourselves. My in-depth research (see the sidebar "Studying Career Change" for an explanation of my methods) leads me to a different conclusion: People most often fail because they go about it all wrong. Indeed, the conventional wisdom on how to change careers is in fact a prescription for how to stay put. The problem lies in our methods, not our motives.

In my study, I saw many people try a conventional approach and then languish for months, if not years. But by taking a different tack, one I came to call the practice of *working identity*, they eventually found their way to brand-new careers. The phrase "working identity," of course, carries two meanings. It is, first, our sense of self in our professional roles, what we convey about ourselves to others and, ultimately, how we live our working lives. But it can also denote action—a process of applying effort to reshape that identity. Working our identity, I found, is a matter of skill, not personality, and therefore can be learned by almost anyone seeking professional renewal. But first we have to be willing to abandon everything we have ever been taught about making sound career decisions.

A Three-Point Plan

We like to think that the key to a successful career change is knowing what we want to do next, then using that knowledge to guide our actions. But studying people in the throes of the career change process (as opposed to afterward, when hindsight is always 20/20) led me to a startling conclusion: Change actually happens the other way around. Doing comes first, knowing second.

Why? Because changing careers means redefining our working identity. Career change follows a first-act-and-then-think sequence because who we are and what we do are tightly connected, the result of years of action; to change that connection, we must also resort to action—exactly what the conventional wisdom cautions us against.

Conventional career change methods—Susan's "logical" CV progression, Harris's networking, and Gary's planning—are all part of what I call the "plan and implement" model

Herminia Ibarra is a professor of organizational behavior at Insead in Fontainebleau, France. Her forthcoming book, *Working Identity: Unconventional Strategies for Reinventing Your Career* (Harvard Business School Press), identifies conditions that enable people to make major career changes.

of change. It goes like this: First, determine with as much clarity and certainty as possible what you really want to do. Next, use that knowledge to identify jobs or fields in which your passions can be coupled with your skills and experience. Seek advice from the people who know you best and from professionals in tune with the market. Then simply implement the resulting action steps. Change is seen as a one-shot deal: The plan-and-implement approach cautions us against making a move before we know exactly where we are going.

It all sounds reasonable, and it is a reassuring way to proceed. Yet my research suggests that proceeding this way will lead to the most disastrous of results, which is to say no result. So if your deepest desire is to remain indefinitely in a career that grates on your nerves or stifles your self-expression, simply adhere to that conventional wisdom, presented below as a foolproof, three-point plan.

Know Thyself

Like Gary McCarthy, most of us are taught to begin a career change with a quest for self-knowledge. Knowing, in theory, comes from self-reflection, in solitary introspection or with the help of standardized questionnaires and certified professionals. Learning whether we are introverted or extroverted, whether we prefer to work in a structured and methodical environment or in chaos, whether we place greater value on impact or income helps us avoid jobs that will again prove unsatisfying. Having reached an understanding of his or her temperament, needs, competencies, core values, and priorities, a person can go out and find a job or organization that matches.

Gary did all these things. Armed with his test results, he researched promising companies and industries and networked with a lot of people to get leads and referrals. He made two lists of possibilities: "conformist" and "nonconformist." But what happened from there, and what consumed 90% of the year he spent looking for a new career, is what the conventional models leave out—a lot of trial and error.

Gary started with several rounds of talking with traditional companies and headhunters. Next, he tried to turn a passion or a hobby into a career: He and his wife wrote a business plan for a wine-tour business. The financials were not great, so they dropped it. Next, he

Studying Career Change

Certain career transitions have been thoroughly studied and are well understood: a move into a position of greater managerial responsibility and organizational status, a transfer to a similar job in a new company or industry, a lateral move into a different work function within a familiar field. But few researchers have investigated how managers and professionals go about making a true change of direction.

My research is an in-depth study of 39 people who changed, or were in the process of trying to change, careers. Determining the magnitude of any work transition is highly subjective. Who, apart from the person who has lived through it, can say whether a shift is radical or incremental? After interviewing dozens of people who were making very different kinds of career moves, I settled on a three-part definition of career change.

Some of the people in my study made significant changes in the context in which they worked, most typically jumping from large, established companies to small, entrepreneurial organizations or to self-employment or between the for-profit and nonprofit sectors. Others made major changes in the content of the work, sometimes leaving occupations, such as medicine, law or academia, that they had trained for extensively. The majority made significant changes in both what they did and where they did it, but most important, all experienced a feeling of having reached a crossroad, one that would require psychological change.

My sample ranged in age from 32 to 51, with an average of 41. I chose this range not to coincide with the infamous midlife crisis but to study a group of people with enough experience in one career to make a shift to another high-stakes endeavor. Sixty-five percent of the participants were men. Almost half of the subjects lived and worked outside the United States, mostly in France and the UK. It was a highly credentialed sample: All had college degrees, and about three-fourths held graduate or professional degrees (business, science, law, and so on). They represented all walks of managerial and professional life, including business management, law, finance, academia, medicine, science, and technology.

Some of the interviews were retrospective, with people who had already completed their changes. With people at earlier stages of the transition, I conducted an average of three interviews over two to three years. The interviews were open-ended, typically beginning with: "Tell me about your career to date." Between the interviews, I had e-mail exchanges and telephone conversations with participants to keep track of their progress. I supplemented this core study with many shorter interviews involving a range of career change professionals, including headhunters, venture capitalists, career counselors, and outplacement specialists.

pursued his true fantasy career: Gary got certified as a scuba instructor and looked into the purchase of a dive operation. He soon learned, though, that his dream job was unlikely to hold his interest over the long term (and thus was not worth the economic sacrifice). So he went back to the headhunters and traditional companies, only to reconfirm that he did not want what they had to offer. Next, he identified entrepreneurs he admired and looked for ways to get his foot in their doors. He explored freelancing, trying to get short-term projects in exciting young companies. But a precise match did not materialize.

Certainly the common practice of looking back over our careers and identifying what we liked and disliked, what we found satisfying and not satisfying, can be a useful tool. But too often this practice is rooted in the profound misconception that it is possible to discover one's "true self," when the reality is that none of us has such an essence. (See the sidebar "Our Many Possible Selves" for a discussion of why one's true self is so elusive.)

Intense introspection also poses the danger that a potential career changer will get stuck in the realm of daydreams. Either the fantasy never finds a match in a real-world, paycheck-producing job or, unlike Gary, we remain emotionally attached to a fantasy career that we do not realize we have outgrown.

We learn who we have become—in practice, not in theory—by testing fantasy and reality, not by "looking inside." Knowing oneself is crucial, but it is usually the outcome of—and not a first input to—the reinvention process. Worse, starting out by trying to identify one's true self often causes paralysis. While we wait for the flash of blinding insight, opportunities pass us by. To launch ourselves anew, we need to get out of our heads. We need to *act*.

Consult Trusted Advisers

If you accept the conventional wisdom that career change begins with self-knowledge and proceeds through an objective scrutiny of the available choices, who should you turn to for

Our Many Possible Selves

What is identity? Most traditional definitions—the ones that form the foundation for most career advice—are based on the notion of an "inner core" or a "true self." By early adulthood, these theories suggest, a person has formed a relatively stable personality structure, defined by his or her aptitudes, preferences, and values. Excavating this true self—often forgotten in a dead-end pursuit of fame, fortune, or social approval—should be the starting point of any career reorientation, according to conventional wisdom. With the appropriate self-knowledge, obtained via introspection and psychological testing, a person can more easily search for the right "match" and avoid the mistakes of the past. This true-self definition corresponds perfectly to the plan-and-implement method—once we find the self, all that remains is execution.

The work of Stanford cognitive psychologist Hazel Markus and other behavioral scientists, however, offers a different definition of identity, one that is more consistent with what I have discovered: We are many selves. And while these selves are defined partly by

our histories, they are defined just as powerfully by our present circumstances and our hopes and fears for the future.

Our possible selves—the images and fantasies we all have about who we hope to become, think we should become, or even fear becoming—are at the heart of the career change process. Although conventional wisdom says pain—a self we fear becoming—is the only driver for change, in reality pain can create paralysis. We change only when we have enticing alternatives that we can feel, touch, and taste. That is why working identity, as a practice, is necessarily a process of experimenting, testing, and learning about our possible selves.

Take Gary McCarthy, the former investment banker and consultant profiled in the main article. The set of possible selves he considered is typical in its number and range. It included a "ditch it all and open a tour-guide business in the south of France with my wife" self; a socially respectable "junior partner" self that his parents would have endorsed; a youthful, outdoorsy, "follow your passion" self who renounced convention and

wanted to open a scuba business; a "responsible spouse and future parent" self who wanted to make good dual-career decisions; a "corporate drone at age 50, full of regrets" self; an "apprentice" self who learned at the elbow of an admired entrepreneur; and a practical, reasonable, "go to a traditional company where I can combine my backgrounds in banking and consulting" self.

Conventional wisdom would say that the scope of his list of possibilities was evidence that he lacked focus and wasn't ready for change. But within the working identity framework, it was precisely this variety that allowed him to find a truly good fit. Certain possible selves are concrete and tangible, defined by the things we do and the company we keep today; others remain vague and fuzzy, existing only in the realm of private dreams, hypothetical possibilities, and abstract ideas. By bringing the possibilities—both desired and feared, present and future—more sharply into focus, we give ourselves a concrete base of experience from which to choose among them.

guidance? Conventional wisdom has it that you should look to those who know you best and those who know the market. Friends and family—with whom you share a long history—can offer insight into your true nature, and they have your best interests at heart; professionals add a dose of pragmatism, keeping you grounded in the realities of the marketplace.

In times of change and uncertainty, we naturally take comfort in our enduring connections with friends and family. But when it comes to reinventing ourselves, the people who know us best are the ones most likely to hinder rather than help us. They may wish to be supportive, but they tend to reinforce—or even desperately try to preserve—the old identities we are trying to shed. Early in his career, Gary discovered that his close circle would not be much help. "I wanted to do something different but was shocked to realize that people were already pigeonholing me," he says. "I tried to brainstorm with friends and family about what other things I might do. All the ideas that came back were a version of 'Well, you could get a middle management job in a finance department of a company.' Or 'You could become a trainee in a management program.'" John Alexander, an investment banker hoping to make a go of fiction writing, reports that he had often discussed his career predicament with his friends and family. "They would tend to say, 'I can see why writing might be interesting, but you've got a very good job, and do you really want to jeopardize that?'"

Mentors and close coworkers, though well meaning, can also unwittingly hold us back. Take Harris Roberts, the health care company director who wanted to assume a general management role. The people around him, who were invested in his staying put, only mirrored his normal doubts about moving outside his comfort zone. His mentors cared about him and held the power to make his desired change a reality. But they made a fence, not a gateway, blocking the moves that would lead to career change. By talking only to people who inhabited his immediate professional world, people whose ideas for him didn't go beyond the four walls, Harris seriously limited himself. Not only did he lack outside market information, but these coworkers could no more let go of their outdated image of a junior Harris than he himself could.

Headhunters and outplacers, today's career change professionals, can keep us tethered to the past just as effectively. We assume, rightly, that they have the market perspective we lack—but we forget that they are in the business of facilitating incremental moves along an established trajectory. At midcareer, however, many people are no longer looking to "leverage past experience in a different setting." They want to invent their own jobs and escape the shackles of corporate convention, in some cases to do something completely different. What Susan Fontaine, the management consultant, experienced is typical: "I found headhunters unhelpful, basically. I would say, 'Here are my skills; what else might I do?' And they kept saying, 'Why don't you move to Andersen?' or, 'Why don't you try Bain?' All they could suggest was exactly the same thing. I kept saying,' I'm quite clear I don't want to do that, and if I did want to do that, I would not come to you. I can do that on my own.'"

So if self-assessment, the advice of close ones, and the counsel of change professionals won't do it, then where can we find support for our reinvention? To make a true break with the past, we need to see ourselves in a new light. We need guides who have been there and can understand where we are going. Reaching outside our normal circles to new people, networks, and professional communities is the best way to both break frame and get psychological sustenance.

Think Big

We like to think that we can leap directly from a desire for change to a single decision that will complete our reinvention—the conventional wisdom would say you shouldn't fool yourself with small, superficial adjustments. But trying to tackle the big changes too quickly can be counterproductive. Just as starting the transition by looking for one's true self can cause paralysis rather than progress, trying to make one big move once and for all can prevent real change.

When Susan Fontaine decided to leave her consulting career, it was with good reason. A single mother of two, she was finding the travel and other demands on her personal life increasingly intolerable. She quit her job and resolved to spend some time exploring her options. That resolve vanished, however,

My research suggests that conventional, reasonable-sounding career change methods will lead to the most disastrous of results, which is to say no result.

when financial pressure coincided with a flattering offer to join the management team of a former client. She accepted the new position only to discover that its demands would be very similar to those of the position she had left. "I thought, 'What have I done?'" she later told me. "I had had the opportunity to leave all that!" By hoping to solve all her problems in one fell swoop, Susan made a change that amounted to no change at all. Two weeks into the new job, she resigned.

As much as we might want to avoid endless procrastination, premature closure is not the answer. It takes time to discover what we truly want to change and to identify the deeply grooved habits and assumptions that are holding us back. The lesson of Susan's story is that trying to make a single bold move can bring us back to square one all too quickly. A longer, less linear transition process may leave us feeling that we are wasting time. But as we will see below, taking smaller steps can allow a richer, more grounded redefinition of our working identity to emerge.

Test and Learn

Your working identity is an amalgam of the kind of work you do, the relationships and organizations that form part of your work life, and the story you tell about why you do what you do and how you arrived at that point. Reshaping that identity, therefore, is a matter of making adjustments to all three of those aspects over time. The adjustments happen tentatively and incrementally, so the process can seem disorderly. In fact, it is a logical process of testing, discovering, and adapting that can be learned by almost anyone seeking professional renewal.

Crafting Experiments

Working identity is defined by what we do, the professional activities that engage us.		Try out new activities and professional roles on a small scale before making a major commitment to a different path.

Shifting Connections

Working identity is also defined by the company we keep, our working relationships, and the professional groups to which we belong.		Develop contacts that can open doors to new worlds, and look for role models and new reference groups to guide and benchmark your progress.

Making Sense

Working identity is also defined by the formative events in our lives and the stories that link who we were and who we will become.		Find or create catalysts and triggers for change, and use them as occasions to rework your life story.

Three Success Stories

Although they floundered, victims of conventional wisdom, Gary McCarthy, Harris Roberts, and Susan Fontaine eventually moved on to a different—and more successful—approach. Gary is now at a media company he admires, working as an internal venture capitalist, a role that allows him to use his skill set in consulting and finance but grants him great creative latitude and total ownership of his results. Harris is president and COO of a growing medical device company and very much involved in setting the strategic direction of his new firm. Susan is working with non-profits, bringing her strategy expertise to this sector and loving her work.

None of them followed a straight and narrow route. Gary dabbled in wine tours and flirted with buying a scuba diving operation before settling on what his wife called a more normal path. Harris had his prized general management role snatched from under him a second time as the result of a corporate restructuring. He considered leaving for a biotech start-up but realized that he simply did not have the appetite for such a risky move. Susan set up temporarily as a freelance consultant, landing traditional consulting projects to pay the bills and using her discretionary time to explore a more varied portfolio of assignments.

Their experience is typical. Nearly everyone who tries to figure out a next career takes a long time to find the one that is truly right. Most career transitions take about three years. It is rarely a linear path: We take two steps forward and one step back, and where we end up often surprises us.

Working Identity

Once we start questioning not just whether we are in the right job or organization today but also what we thought we wanted for the future, the job search methods we have all been taught fail us. But that doesn't mean we must resign ourselves to a random process governed by factors outside our control—life crisis that forces us to reprioritize, an unexpected job offer. There is an alternative method that works according to a different logic than the plan-and-implement approach. Gary, Harris, and Susan, as well as many other successful career changers I have observed, shared this method, which I call the "test and learn" model of change. During times of transition—when our possible selves are shifting wildly—the only way to create change is by putting our possible identities into practice, working and crafting them until they are sufficiently grounded in experience to guide more decisive steps. (See the sidebar "Test and Learn.")

The test-and-learn approach recognizes that the only way to counter uncertainty and resist the pull of the familiar is to make alternative futures more vivid, more tangible, and more doable. We acquired our old identities in practice. Likewise, we redefine them, in practice, by crafting experiments, shifting connections, and making sense of the changes we are going through. These three common practices lie at the heart of the most disparate of career changes, lending logic to what can look like chance occurrences and disorderly behavior.

Crafting Experiments. By far the biggest mistake people make when trying to change careers is delaying the first step until they have settled on a destination. This error is undermining because the only way we figure out what we really want to do is by giving it a try. Understandably, most people are reluctant to leap into the unknown. We must test our fantasies—otherwise, they remain just that. I discovered that most people create new working identities on the side at first, by getting involved in extracurricular ventures and weekend projects.

Crafting experiments refers to the practice of creating these side projects. Their great advantage is that we can try out new professional roles on a limited scale without compromising our current jobs or having to leap into new positions too quickly. In almost every instance of successful change that I have observed, the person had already been deeply engaged in the new career for quite some time.

There are many ways to set up experiments that work. Newly resolved to explore a range of possibilities, Susan took freelancing assignments in her old line of work and did pro bono work for charities as her lifeline to get her through this difficult period. Through that work, she began to develop contacts that led to paid charity consulting. Gradually, she became immersed in nonprofits, a sector she had never expected to find a career in. And she found herself enjoying freelancing. Today, she is working with the largest UK consulting firm that specializes in charities, and she has this to say: "All I hope is that I never again make the mistake of jumping before giving myself the chance to explore what I really want to do."

Other people use temporary assignments, outside contracts, advisory work, and moonlighting to get experience or build skills in new industries. Thanks to a temporary stint at the helm of his division, Harris got over his fear, which had silently plagued him for years, that he lacked the finance and cross-functional background necessary to be a good general manager. This concrete experience, more than any amount of self-reflection, helped him envision himself as a general manager. Taking courses or picking up training and credentials in a new area is still another way of experimenting. For many of the people in my study, an executive program, sabbatical, or extended vacation improved their capacity to move in a new direction. These breaks are powerful because they force us to step back from the daily routine while engaging us with new people and activities.

Shifting Connections. Consider how common it is for employees to say of their companies, "There is no one here I want to be like." At midcareer, our desire for change is rarely about only the work we do; it is perhaps more importantly about changing our working relationships so they are more satisfying and inspiring. Shifting connections refers to the practice of finding people who can help us see and grow into our new selves. For most successful career changers I have observed, a guiding figure or new professional community helped to light the way and cushion the eventual leap.

Finding a new job always requires networking outside our usual circles. We get ideas and job leads by branching out. Gary, for example, used his alumni and company networks quite successfully. It was an ex-employee of his company—someone he didn't know personally—who got him the temporary project at his current company. But what clinched his decision, what made this job different from all the other conformist roles he had considered, was the opportunity to work for a role model he had long admired and from whom he could learn the ropes.

Seeking refuge in close working relationships is natural in times of change and uncertainty. But Harris made a classic mistake in turning to an old mentor, Alfred, who was too invested in Harris remaining the unsure protégé to give him room to grow. Harris's way out of this "codependent" relationship came via a person he had met casually at a professional conference. Gerry, the company founder who later hired Harris as his COO, initially approached Harris for regulatory advice. Eventually, they developed an informal consulting relationship. In Gerry, Harris found a person who believed in his potential as a general manager and offered a different kind of close, interdependent working relationship: "It was such a contrast to my relationship with Alfred," Harris says. "It's not as paternal. Gerry knows things I need to learn—things that re late to creative financing, ways to raise money—but he also needs to learn from me. He doesn't know how to run a company, and I do. He's looking to me to teach him what's necessary to develop an organization, to build a foundation. I think I can learn a lot from Gerry, but it's a more mature and more professional relationship than I had with Alfred."

To make a break with the past, we must venture into unknown networks—and not just for job leads. Often it is strangers who are best equipped to help us see who we are becoming.

Making Sense. In the middle of the confusion about which way to go, many of us hope for one event that will clarify everything, that will transform our stumbling moves into a coherent trajectory. Julio Gonzales, a doctor trying to leave the practice of medicine, put it like this: "I was waiting for an epiphany—I wake up in the middle of the night and the Angel of Mercy tells me *this* is what I should do." The third working identity practice, making sense, refers to creating our own triggers for change: infusing events—the momentous and the mundane—with special meaning and weaving them into a story about who we are becoming.

Every person who has changed careers has a story about the moment of truth. For John Alexander, the would-be author I've mentioned, the moment of truth came when, on a whim, he visited an astrologer. To his surprise, the first thing she said to him was, "I'm glad I haven't been *you* for the last two or three years. You have been undergoing a painful internal tug-of-war between two opposing factions. One side wants stability, economic well-being, and social status, and the other craves artistic expression, maybe as a writer or an impresario. You may wish to believe that there can be reconciliation between these two. I tell you, there cannot be." Another career changer, a woman who had grown increasingly frustrated as an executive in a high-tech start-up, said, "One day my husband just asked me, 'Are you happy? If you are, that's great. But you don't *look* happy.' His question prompted me to reconsider what I was doing."

It would be easy to believe from such accounts that career changes have their geneses in such moments. But the moment of insight is an effect, not a cause, of change. Across my many interviews, a striking discovery was that such moments tended to occur late in the transition process, only after much trial and tribulation. Rather than catalyzing change, defining moments helped people make sense of changes that had long been unfolding.

Trigger events don't just jolt us out of our habitual routines, they are the necessary pegs on which to hang our reinvention stories. Arranging life events into a coherent story is one of the subtlest, yet most demanding, challenges of career reinvention. To reinvent oneself is to rework one's story. At the start of a career transition, when all we have is a laundry list of diffuse ideas, it unsettles us that we have no story. It disturbs us to find so many different options appealing, and we worry that the same self who once chose what we no longer want to do might again make a bad choice. Without a story that explains why we must change, the external audience to whom we are selling our reinvention remains dubious, and we, too, feel unsettled and uncertain.

Good stories develop in the telling and retelling, by being put into the public sphere even before they are fully formed. Instead of being embarrassed about having visited an astrologer, for example, John told everyone his story and even wrote about it in a newspaper column. The closer he got to finding his creative outlet, the more the episode made sense and the less often his story elicited the "Why would you want to do that?" reaction. By making public declarations about what we seek and about the common thread that binds our old and new selves, we clarify our intentions and improve our ability to enlist others' support.

The Road Now Taken

Most of us know what we are trying to escape: the lockstep of a narrowly defined career, inauthentic or unstimulating work, numbing corporate politics, a lack of time for life outside of work. Finding an alternative that truly fits, like finding one's mission in life, cannot be accomplished overnight. It takes time, perseverance, and hard work. But effort isn't enough; a sound method and the skill to put it into practice are also required.

The idea of working one's identity flies in the face of everything we have always been told about choosing careers. It asks us to devote the greater part of our time and energy to action rather than reflection, to doing instead of planning. It tells us to give up the search for a ten-point plan and to accept instead a crooked path. But what appears to be a mysterious, road-to-Damascus process is actually a learning-by-doing practice that any of us can adopt. We start by taking action.

Reprint R0212B
To order, see the next page
or call 800-988-0886 or 617-783-7500
or go to www.hbr.org

How to Stay Stuck in the Wrong Career

Further Reading

ARTICLES

A Second Career: The Possible Dream
by Harry Levinson
Harvard Business Review
May–June 1983
Product no. 83307

Levinson describes an approach to midlife career change that blends elements of "testing and learning" with "planning and implementing." He begins by considering a version of working identity he calls **ego ideal**: your idealized image of your future self, including goals you'd like to achieve. He then explains how to clarify your ego ideal by asking a series of probing questions, such as, "What lifetime experiences have I found most gratifying?" and "What kinds of achievements do I admire?"

Next Levinson suggests ways to identify the activities and work environments appropriate for your ego ideal. Finally, he considers the unique concerns facing midlife career changers, such as family responsibilities, potential loss of status, and the feelings of loss that accompany major job changes.

Reawakening Your Passion for Work
by Richard Boyatzis, Annie McKee, and Daniel Goleman
Harvard Business Review
April 2002
Product no. 9659

These authors shift gears to executives who are at the apex of their careers and begin to feel that something is missing from their work lives. Addressing this feeling is essential for renewing their energy, creativity, and commitment—and their ability to inspire others.

The article emphasizes the importance of **knowing when it's time for a change**. Signals include: 1) *"I feel trapped."* Once-meaningful work seems less meaningful. You're restless but can't change or articulate what's wrong. 2) *"I feel bored."* Life seems to lack satisfying work, intellectual stimulation, and fun. You're just

"going through the motions." 3) *"I can't ignore the call."* You're strongly drawn to a new mission, such as becoming a teacher.

BOOK

Working Identity: Unconventional Strategies for Reinventing Your Career
by Herminia Ibarra
Harvard Business School Press
November 2002
Product no. 7788

This book expands on the ideas in "How to Stay Stuck in the Wrong Career." The author acknowledges the powerful pull of the familiar and the difficulty in moving away from a current profession in which we've invested long years and intense effort. Based on her research on professionals and managers in transition, Ibarra outlines the "test and learn" process of career reinvention and provides examples of people who have successfully used the three tactics described in her HBR article.

She shares additional suggestions for deciding when to abandon your current path and follow a new one, crafting and executing "identity experiments," creating "small wins" that keep your momentum going, connecting with new role models and mentors who can ease the transition, and surviving the rocky period between career identities.

Harvard Business Review ⚜

To Order

For *Harvard Business Review* reprints and subscriptions, call 800-988-0886 or 617-783-7500. Go to www.hbr.org

For customized and quantity orders of *Harvard Business Review* article reprints, call 617-783-7626, or e-mail customizations@hbsp.harvard.edu

Harvard Business Review

www.hbr.org

Chances are that you will be fired at least once. When that day comes, will your reaction hurt you or help you?

The Right Way to Be Fired

by Laurence J. Stybel and Maryanne Peabody

Included with this full-text *Harvard Business Review* article:

Reprint R0107F

The Right Way to Be Fired

The Idea in Brief

Even if you're a top-notch executive in the best of times, you can still lose your job. But can you lose it the *right* way?

For some executives, getting fired is cause for lashing out, sinking into depression, or silently retreating. But these responses make it difficult to generate new opportunities—and can destroy careers.

How can you avoid these termination traps and make the best of being fired? First, get rid of the "tenure mind-set"—that falsely comforting sense that your organization will take care of you until you formally retire. Instead, adopt the "assignment mind-set"—seeing each job as a stepping-stone, a temporary project in your long-term career.

Then, take steps to control how you're fired—and how you respond. The payoff? You position yourself for excellent new opportunities *and* you make a great catch for your next employer. *You're* in control

The Idea in Practice

TERMINATION TRAPS

Executives risk falling into these traps when losing a job:

TRAP	WHO'S MOST SUSCEPTIBLE	WHAT HAPPENS
Lost Identity	Founders, senior execs, longtime company leaders who've accumulated power and have "become" their jobs.	They **fight back**—lashing out against former employers and branding themselves as people no one wants to work with.
Lost Family	Leaders in companies with high emotional intensity where people consider colleagues family.	They **mourn**—sinking into bitterness and depression, becoming unattractive candidates for future positions.
Lost Ego	Introverts with top positions in areas requiring little outside interaction (e.g., accounting, engineering).	They **fade away**—neglecting to negotiate decent severance and refusing to network to generate new opportunities.

ASSUME YOU'LL BE FIRED—AND LAY THE RIGHT GROUNDWORK

How to manage the possibility of being fired? Accept the impermanence of your job, and take these systematic approaches to your next move:

- **Insert a termination clause in your employment contract**—Counterintuitive, yes, but it's your best hedge against a bitter exit. You're never as attractive as the day you sign your contract.

- **Schedule network phone calls**—Make networking a disciplined, regular part of doing business. Keep your web of professional contacts intact.

- **Raise your visibility**—Conduct your own public-relations campaign, keeping a strong industry profile. Serve on for-profit boards in and outside your industry. Volunteer for trade associations' externally oriented committees.

- **Watch for exit signs**—Getting fired should not come as a surprise. If your firm hustles people out the door, raise your own guard. If the company itself has an exit plan, find out how it affects your position. Consult with trusted, seasoned advisers who can alert you to potential changes.

- **Volunteer to be terminated**—if the firm's exit strategy includes you. This makes you the actor, rather than the one acted upon.

Chances are that you will be fired at least once. When that day comes, will your reaction hurt you or help you?

The Right Way to Be Fired

by Laurence J. Stybel and Maryanne Peabody

Even in the best of times, executives get fired, and in the worst, they get fired with disquieting frequency. Indeed, as the economy softens, you only have to glance at the newspaper to see layoffs left, right, and center, mainly to cut costs. You can be a top performer today and still lose your job. The question is: Can you lose it the right way?

For 22 years, we have worked closely with more than 500 senior executives in dozens of industries to manage their careers in good times and in bad. Over and over, we have observed how executives react to being fired or laid off. The majority handle termination with dignity, even elegance. They negotiate handsome severance packages, part with their employers on amicable terms, and position themselves for their next assignments. Yet some executives take actions that subsequently backfire, setting the stage for difficulty in procuring new jobs—and even destroying their careers.

What differentiates fired employees who make the best of their situations from those

who do not? One answer is mind-set. Virtually every executive feels shock and anger upon losing a job, but those who rebound swiftly have usually absorbed what we call an "assignment mentality"; they see each job as a stepping-stone, a temporary career-building project. That's good, because most corporate boards and CEOs have this mind-set, too, a continuing phenomenon that emerged about 20 years ago. Most leaders see an executive in the ranks—even the best performers—as filling an assignment. When it's over—for strategic or financial reasons so is the executive's tenure with the company.

On an intellectual level, most executives know that the assignment mentality rules. Even so, some allow that reality to recede in their minds; it's only human nature. Then they get fired or are laid off and, like clockwork, fall into one of three traps. The first is the "lost identity" trap. Executives in this group have, over months or years, allowed themselves to "become" their jobs. Unable to imagine their companies existing without them or themselves existing without their companies, they react to termination with rage, even vengeance. The second is the "lost family" trap, the province of executives who believe that their coworkers are more than that—dear friends, even a second family. Under these circumstances, termination becomes painful estrangement, with attendant feelings of betrayal and sorrow. Finally, there is the "lost ego" trap, in which executives silently retreat from the company without negotiating fair termination packages and disappear into troughs of silent despair that make them reluctant to reach for the next opportunities.

We'll examine these traps, all of which can arise from being fired or laid off, in the following pages and then turn to a few strategies for making a dignified departure. But first, a few observations about the assignment mentality itself.

Which Mind-Set Do You Have?

The assignment model common in most companies today got its start in project-oriented industries—such as the arts, sports, agriculture, construction, and consulting. In these arenas, work comes and goes; individuals are contracted as needed; and work groups are continually assembled, altered, and dissolved. The assignment model presupposes the existence of "assignment executives"—people hired for two to six years to guide and implement a company's strategy. Sometimes, a company itself may be on assignment, in the sense that its end is foreseeable: For example, a company faced with a short product life cycle, tough competition, or an unforgiving investment community may develop a corporate exit strategy. Such an exit strategy might be to increase shareholder value by 50% and then engineer an initial public offering or an acquisition by a larger competitor. Once this strategy is successful, a new group of senior managers replaces the outgoing one.

Although the assignment model is real, it is rarely discussed. A mythic belief lives alongside it in the minds of most employees. This is the "tenure mind-set"—the comforting sense that an organization willingly parts with valued employees only when they formally retire. It has long been dead in corporate America, although most companies won't openly admit it. After all, letting employees

know that their jobs are finite would make them feel disposable and would hurt recruiting efforts. For this reason, most companies perpetuate the tenure myth, particularly in corporate literature. Annual reports and other accounts, filled with glowing language about career paths, continually work to persuade employees that companies take long-term views of their career development.

Most of the time, the assignment and tenure mind-sets coexist peacefully. Externally hired CEOs truly understand that their jobs are pure assignments, because very specific termination and severance clauses are written into the employment contracts. For everyone else, the assignment nature of the job may not be clearly understood. Indeed, it's easy to ignore, even to deny. Moreover, senior executives tend to believe their own jobs are the most secure. And it isn't unusual for a founder, a CEO, or an executive promoted from within to be lulled into the tenure mind-set. When the company's exit strategy dictates a departure and sets in motion a collision between the two mind-sets, disillusionment can emerge and executives can fall into one of the three traps.

Caught in the Quagmire

When terminated suddenly, even the most widely admired and competent executives can be overcome by anger and grief. Saddled by these emotional responses, they may take actions they later regret. Let's take a closer look at these three traps.

The Lost Identity Trap. The people most susceptible to this trap are likely to have been with a company for some time; their jobs may have been cut short due to a sudden change in course or a pressing financial crisis. Such people often include founders and senior executives who have achieved positions of power through promotion. In the day-to-day demands of doing their jobs, executives who fall into this trap have nurtured the strong sense that they are indispensable; they may have heard as much from investors or board members. Confronted with sudden job loss, they fall apart and often lash out against the former company—now rife with "enemies."

Consider Fred, a 31-year-old engineer who received his degree from MIT and then spent three years working for a large computer manufacturer. There, he developed a key

Laurence J. Stybel and **Maryanne Peabody** are the founding partners of Stybel Peabody Lincolnshire, a Boston-based consulting firm. Their Web site is www.boardoptions.com.

technology that allowed companies to tap into their large databases via the Internet. After inventing the software, Fred decided to found a company with his own sweat equity; in time, he accepted funding from a venture capital firm with the understanding that he would be surrendering control of day-to-day operations to one of the venture partners. The partner said that Fred's continued presence was extremely important and that he hoped that Fred would consider assuming the role of chairman. Eager to finance his company, Fred agreed.

Eventually, the VC firm hired a permanent CEO, a 54-year-old man who had plenty of managerial experience but who lacked the technical skills that Fred so prized in himself. When he wanted to drive home a point, the CEO called Fred "son"; in response, Fred would mutter, "I already have a father." One day, the CEO and the VC met with Fred and fired him.

A few weeks later, Fred told us angrily, "I was kicked out of my own company." By then, Fred had done a lot of damage. In the days after his termination, he phoned each of the partners of the VC firm and accused them of betrayal. He refused to pass on his operational or engineering knowledge to anyone within the company. And when an industry analyst called to find out what had happened, Fred "secretly" confided his anger and frustration. Soon, word of Fred's unprofessional behavior circulated in both the large software industry and the small VC community. Eventually, Fred created a new start-up software company but, stamped as a person no one wanted to make deals with, was unable to secure further VC funding.

The Lost Family Trap. This trap is most prevalent among people working in fields like marketing or magazine publishing or within start-ups—all environments of high emotional intensity. Employees in such organizations can form tight-knit, emotional bonds, just as troops in combat do. These bonds can become so close that relationships with people outside work may seem dull.

Like the main character in the 1970s sitcom *The Mary Tyler Moore Show*, executives with such intense connections can make work the emotional center of their universe. Projecting familial roles upon colleagues, who become surrogate parents, siblings, aunts, or uncles, these executives suffer grief when, on termination, the "old gang" suddenly grows distant. But who can blame the coworkers? Suffering from survivor guilt and perhaps worrying about losing their own jobs, they're instinctively turning away from the person in pain. The coworkers, too, are in shock. Executives, however, caught emotionally in the lost family trap, can't see this. They feel as if friendships have been severed and they've been rejected. As a result, they sink into bitterness and depression.

Justine was the CEO of a consumer goods manufacturing company that had once dominated its marketplace. A 15-year veteran of her company, she was an energetic workaholic who felt alive only when she was at work. Justine loved her husband and children, but she found family life mundane compared with the adrenaline-pumping game of business. Over time, however, the company began losing market share. Although the members of the board liked Justine, they felt that the company needed to go in a completely new direction by taking its manufacturing offshore; Justine fought this idea because it meant shutting down facilities and laying off beloved workers. The board, impatient to reposition the company to take advantage of new opportunities, unanimously voted to let Justine go and replace her with a new CEO.

On an intellectual level, Justine understood that anyone can be fired. As head of the company, she had arranged enough terminations to know how the game is played. But upon being fired herself, Justine believed she had lost not only her job and income but also the de facto family of which she believed herself the matriarch. When she reached out to her former subordinates, whom she had protected and befriended, they did not have time to meet her for drinks or dinner and seemed uninterested in how she was faring. The truth was that her "family" was afraid to go near her for fear that merely associating with Justine would bring them to the board's attention.

Unable to hide her depression and bitterness, Justine became an unattractive candidate. Recruiters felt she had failed to manage her board properly and hadn't rebounded from an event that should have been predictable. Unable to find work, Justine purchased a franchise retail operation, whose employees became a replacement family—and from which she could never be fired.

Fired executives who rebound swiftly have usually absorbed an assignment mentality; they see each job as a stepping-stone, a temporary career-building project.

The Lost Ego Trap. Executives who fall into the lost ego trap, in our observations, tend to be introverts. Such people work very effectively in areas of the company such as accounting and finance, R&D, manufacturing, or engineering, which don't demand high levels of socialization with outside constituencies. After being unexpectedly terminated, these executives tend to withdraw.

Consider Frank, a CFO for a retail company with $50 million in sales. As a child, Frank was shy and had few friends; although he loved playing the piano, he never enjoyed public performance. After majoring in math in college, Frank earned his CPA and followed a career in finance, eventually attaining the rank of CFO. He became the acting head of the company when the CEO, after a bitter divorce, escaped on his sailboat to cruise around the world and enjoy an extended vaca-tion on a tropical island. Although Frank was competent enough to earn the owner's trust during this long sabbatical, he was not able to prevent a loss of market share when the economy hit tough times. The fall in the company's fortunes forced the CEO to cut short his holiday; upon his return, he fired Frank and resumed control of the business with an eye toward selling it.

Although he had been with the company for 12 years, Frank reacted to the news of his termination and scant severance without a complaint and quietly left, not wanting to make a fuss. It never occurred to him to consult an attorney skilled in severance negotiations for help in procuring a more generous termination package. Every book he read on job hunting recommended networking, but he just couldn't do it; he felt that the books were telling him to be someone he wasn't. In-

Auf Wiedersehen: How To Fire Right

Every industry boasts companies with tra-ditions of never rehiring people who leave, regardless of how well those employees perform. But given the growth of the assign-ment mind-set within corporations, the un-precedented ease of movement between companies, and the difficulty of attracting ex-cellent employees, it no longer makes sense to slam the door behind departed workers who have been solid performers. After all, such employees do not simply vanish into the night. They go to professional meetings, where they can openly discuss their exit treatment with prospective recruits. Cus-tomers, strategic partners, distributors, or acquisition candidates may hire them. And once the noncompete clauses in their em-ployment contracts expire, they might even decide to work for a competitor.

Many companies usher employees out the door with minimal termination packages, even sending them off under a cloud of hu-miliation. We call these "goodbye" termina-tions, because they deal in finality. In one goodbye termination, a CEO who had had a disagreement with the board was fired, al-though the company's press release claimed he had resigned. The chairman then issued an internal memo stating that the board had forced the CEO to resign. Employees saw the ashenfaced CEO clean out his desk and de-part under the gaze of the HR vice president. Not surprisingly, morale within the company dropped precipitously, and several valued employees also quit.

A much better alternative to the goodbye termination is what we call the "auf Wieder-sehen" (German for "until we see you again") termination. An auf Wiedersehen departure assumes that the company will meet the de-parting employee again in another context and thus conducts the termination as re-spectfully as possible. There are several ad-vantages to this approach. First, by making an effort to preserve the employee's dignity and goodwill, the company decreases the chance of a backlash from the employee or of a sullied reputation for its act. Second, when there is a poor fit between an individual and a company, an auf Wiedersehen exit makes it easier for the employee to leave (or even quit) without causing trauma to the com-pany or himself.

In addition, auf Wiedersehen terminations make it possible to re-recruit top-performing alumni. This makes excellent financial sense. According to the Corporate Leadership Coun-cil, it costs 176% of base salary to recruit and train a new IT professional and 241% of base salary to recruit and train a new middle man-ager. When alumni are re-recruited, costs drop to almost zero because companies don't have to pay search firms, interview candi-dates, train employees, or get them ramped up for productivity.

By keeping accurate performance records on past employees and staying in touch with excellent alumni, companies can also reduce the possibility of mis-hire, thus saving time and money. McKinsey, for example, sponsors alumni programs such as special breakfasts and on-line directories that allow former em-ployees to keep in touch with the company and one another. Since alumni are also share-holders, the strong alumnishareholder base has helped attract and retain shareholders during economic downturns.

Using an auf Wiedersehen termination pol-icy doesn't necessarily mean that companies must spend huge amounts on termination benefits; it merely requires that companies treat departing employees with the same re-spect when they leave as they received when they entered. Your pay policies should also be consistent. In comparisons with your competition, don't brag that you pay at the 75th percentile for new hires but at the 50th percentile for terminations. Pay policies and termination policies are two sides of one coin called "how people are treated."

stead of reaching out to acquaintances or taking advantage of professional networks, he relied on third parties such as recruiters or on electronic job boards to find his next position; but these efforts produced few results.

Finally, an opportunity developed with a company 150 miles away from his home. Frank listened lackadaisically as the recruiter described the position. He was already conjuring the negative aspects of the deal. "I'll have to pull the kids out of school and away from all their friends," he thought. "My wife will have to quit the job she loves. We'll have to sell our wonderful home in an uncertain housing market." Frank told the recruiter he would think about it and hung up. But rather than balancing the imagined negatives with the job's prospective benefits—the stable and growing company, a generous relocation package, the excellent position with an equity

stake—Frank focused only on the downsides, which combined into an excuse to turn down the prospect without further consideration. Eventually, he accepted a far less promising position within ten miles of his house.

Exiting with Aplomb

Executives can fall into these traps—of fighting back, mourning, or fading away—when they are reacting to sudden or unexpected events. Better, of course, to be prepared, and in a moment, we'll talk about how to do that. But first, here's a piece of tactical advice. When fired or being laid off, follow the old saying and count to 100 to cool down. That is, resist the impulse to say the first thing that comes into your mind. In fact, try not to say much of anything. Contact an attorney who negotiates severance packages for senior executives. Do not call colleagues, send e-mails, or speak to

Do You Need an Agent?

Consider the following scenario: A recruiter calls you about a "fantastic" opportunity with another company, but you are too busy to give it serious attention. So you propose an alternative. "I want to give this opportunity the consideration it deserves," you say. "Given the demands of my current job, it would not be fair to my company to spend time with you. Let me give you the phone number of my agent. She understands what would be a good fit for me. My agent will do the initial screening. If the answer is yes, then we can talk in more detail. If it's no, I will be glad to refer you to others."

Tiger Woods benefits from having an agent, but a CEO? As far-fetched as it sounds, executive agents are part of a growing industry of coaches. The reason is simple. CEOs must focus their full attention on their current jobs, but in so doing, they forget to manage their careers. As a result, when assignments end, they can find themselves grasping at opportunities rather than making strategic moves.

A CEO agent helps clients with career strategy, presentation skills, image building, networking, and employment and salary negotiations. He or she also helps to screen job opportunities, even to manage money or

save face in difficult situations. But is an executive agent necessary? As partners in an executive search, coaching, and outplacement firm, we can say, "Absolutely not." This kind of professional help makes little sense for extremely senior executives—CEOs like Jack Welch or Michael Dell, for example—who are very public symbols of their enterprises. Many groups within their corporations—such as the corporate public relations and investor relations departments, who keep the CEO's name in the public eye—already do some of the work of CEO agents.

Nor are CEOs who are between assignments good candidates for agents. A CEO agent manages an employed professional's long-term career; the first priority of any job candidate is to focus on securing the next assignment, and an outplacement firm would provide a sharper focus for such an individual. Outplacement services are usually provided to senior executives as part of termination packages and thus do not require personal expense.

Nevertheless, a CEO agent can play an important role, for example, in helping to negotiate the gray area of getting from one assignment to another. Eight months before the expiration of a CEO contract, a board may

begin informal discussions about whether to renew the contract and may use a retained search firm to delicately explore alternatives. At the same time, a CEO's own agent can quietly explore new options. When the company and the CEO sit down to renegotiate the employment contract, both sides benefit from a clear sense of market conditions.

A CEO agent may do the legwork to manage an individual's reputation—that intangible asset that defines an executive's individual worth. One time-consuming aspect of reputation management is networking; focused on the demands of the job, an executive may lack the time to keep the network "warm." Consider Phil, a CEO with a network of 850 business contacts. He would reach out to his network only when he needed to find his next assignment; because he didn't otherwise maintain contact or contribute to committees or associations, he became known as a taker rather than as a giver. Phil commissioned a CEO agent to keep his network warm by sending quarterly personal letters, cards, and relevant articles to his contacts; Phil only signed the letters. As a result, the time he spent looking for a new position between assignments shrank from an average of six months to three.

reporters. In the next 48 hours, people will be contacting you. Say nothing until the severance contract has been signed. It is also important that your spouse or partner stick to whatever "official story" is being developed about you and the company.

That's the short-term fix. Now let's explore long-term strategies for departing correctly. These strategies all involve a proactive—even calculated—approach to termination. They also require adoption of the assignment mind-set: by remaining conscious of the impermanence of their jobs, executives will avoid merely reacting and can adopt systematic approaches to the next move.

Rhonda exemplifies an executive who handled her termination the right way. As a child, she had been raised to believe the adage, "If you take care of the company, the company will take care of you." After completing her

MBA, she moved to San Francisco and worked at a mid-sized software company. When she and all her colleagues lost their jobs during an acquisition, Rhonda reevaluated her tenure mind-set. The experience persuaded her that the familiar adage was no longer tenable, and she learned to treat successive opportunities as moves toward her career goal of becoming a successful CEO.

Eventually, a new e-commerce venture with a focus on distribution hired Rhonda as its CEO. A top-tier VC firm had proffered the first financing round of $3 million and also promised a second round of $7 million. Rhonda—now armed with assignment thinking—negotiated a one-year severance package at full pay as part of the employment contract. Soon afterward, she began growing the company, and the VC partner expressed satisfaction with her efforts. But instead of nurs-

---

A CEO agent can help, too, to ensure that an individual's public reputation remains strong. According to the public relations firm Burson-Marsteller, 45% of a company's reputation rests on that of its CEO. This percentage has increased almost 14% since 1997. Moreover, 95% of analysts who select stock use CEO reputation as a key decision point.

A CEO agent sometimes acts as a career coach, a person familiar with your industry and company who can serve as a trusted, impartial sounding board and work behind the scenes to help you be more effective on the job. A coach is typically an experienced businessperson who, over the years, has developed a gift for navigating business dynamics and with whom the executive develops a close, one-on-one relationship. If, for example, an executive feels she's been given a cold shoulder by someone in the organization with whom she thought she had a good relationship, a coach can help her backtrack through communications to discern possible sources of contention. Or a coach might help an executive discover ways to sell an idea to various constituents within a company, such as strategizing on how to acquire ownership of other parts of a company while the executive maintains a focus on the core aspects of his or her job.

An agent can also supply an executive with a career management infrastructure—public relations professionals to generate a visibility program, administrative staff to keep a network warm, attorneys specializing in employment contract negotiation, financial planners, and outplacement consultants. An agent might even pair an executive with a theater director to assist with an important "performance."

As with any consulting arrangement, an executive who uses an agent should proceed with caution. Here's how.

Depend on excellent references. CEO agents are difficult to find; good ones work strictly by referral. Other CEOs, or contacts in professions that use agents (sports, publishing, media), may be able to refer you to good ones. A few search firms also provide such services. Don't forget to seek help from associations such as the Young Presidents' Organization or Renaissance Executive Forums.

Ask hard questions. Before entering into a relationship with a CEO agent, hold an exploratory meeting or two during which you ask specific questions about how the agent would help manage your career for the long term. It's also important to have an open discussion about potential conflicts of interest, because the agent may know things about your company that you don't. If, for example, the agent works for a search firm that already has a relationship with your company, it's possible that the agent could

be hired to find your successor. To circumvent problems, you and your agent should outline any potential conflicts of interest that either of you can imagine. And if, for any reason, the agent is not on your ethical wavelength, pass.

Understand the arrangement. Don't hire a CEO agent for a onetime transaction. Like your CPA, financial planner, or attorney, your agent is a long-term valued adviser you expect to work with over many years. He or she must be available to you 24/7 to help you with specific work-related and career management issues; it's also wise to include your agent in occasional family discussions about plans and goals. Like professional recruiters and other personal consultants, a CEO agent is hired on retainer, typically charging 5% of the executive's cash compensation, with a $15,000 minimum yearly fee.

Set realistic goals. Work together with your agent to develop six-month and one-year game plans with pragmatic goals. You want to make discernable progress in expanding your visibility, but don't expect miracles. If you are an unknown CEO from a small firm, you probably won't be sitting on the board of a *Fortune* 500 company within three months. Before the annual contract comes up for renewal, meet with your agent to evaluate the year's accomplishments.

ing illusions of permanence, Rhonda kept a weather eye out for signs of the company's approaching exit strategy. She likened her assignment to "parachuting onto a sailboat during a typhoon—I just landed with my hands on the tiller and went from there." Aware of the perilousness of e-commerce ventures, she cultivated her network for the day when she would need it. She served on two corporate boards, one a computer hardware company and the other a wireless communications company, and spent one night every two weeks staying in touch by phone with top business contacts. These were upbeat conversations; she never complained to other executives about her work.

In the spring of 2000, when the Internet bubble burst, the VC partner announced that not only would his firm not put in the $7 million but that it also wanted the whole operation shut down as soon as possible. Of course, Rhonda was angry at the partner for reneging on his promise. But she kept her negative feelings to herself; they passed soon enough, for she was well positioned for the next assignment. The venture capitalist was so impressed by Rhonda's behavior that he wrote a glowing letter of recommendation that complemented her own efforts to procure a new assignment as CEO of a new distribution company with ample financing and a strong market position.

The single most important key to Rhonda's success was her assignment mentality. Although the tenure mind-set had felt natural and comforting to her, she understood that even the most desirable job today is finite. She also understood that she was responsible for crafting her own exit strategy.

In managing current assignments and protecting options for the future, executives can follow Rhonda's example by adopting the following strategies. While not surprising or new, these tasks can be forgotten or postponed by executives too enmeshed in day-to-day work to take care of their careers. And these tactics can prove invaluable during termination.

Insert a termination clause in your employment contract. A new hire is never more attractive to the company than on the day before signing an employment contract; that's when you best control the terms of your employment. If you are newly hired or in the process of being promoted to a position that requires signing a new employment or confidentiality contract, it's possible to build your exit terms into the agreement. Like a prenuptial agreement that protects both sides if a marriage is dissolved, the insertion of such a clause at the time of hire feels completely counterintuitive. Nevertheless, it's your best hedge against a bitter exit. Hire a lawyer with experience in employment contract negotiation to insert clauses that will provide a satisfactory exit package in the event of termination.

Schedule network calls. Make networking a discipline, not a catch-as-catch-can activity. In an assignment-driven world, keeping one's network of professional acquaintances intact is time-consuming, but it's a critical cost of doing business. The importance of networking is obvious—which may be why managers, who sometimes put their own career needs on hold, rarely think of it. Unless network calls are explicitly scheduled and rigorously carried out, they can remain mere intentions. A biweekly calendar note reminds you to get in touch with the important people in your network—especially those with their own strong networks such as valued advisers to CEOs or partners within law, consulting, or accounting firms.

Raise your visibility—by stealth. Most executives understand that if they conduct personal self-branding PR campaigns, their companies will automatically fire them; the only person with official sanction to "represent" the company is likely to be the CEO. On occasion, your company's public relations team may be able to provide you with speaking engagements or bylined articles in trade publications; but such opportunities can be rare.

That's where stealth comes in. You may not be able to talk to reporters, but you can certainly raise your visibility with other professionals. You can serve on for-profit boards, at least one of which should be in an industry other than your own. This is so important that we routinely suggest adding a clause requiring board service into an employment contract. In addition to garnering useful perspectives from peers in other arenas, serving on industry boards expands the network both within and beyond one's core business—making it possible to move into new companies and indus-

By remaining conscious of the impermanence of their jobs, executives can avoid merely reacting and can adopt systematic approaches to the next move.

tries later on. You can also play a selective and strategic leadership role in a trade association. By volunteering for externally oriented committees—such as membership, marketing, legislative affairs, or programs—you'll be able to get in front of outside constituencies while retaining a strong industry profile.

Watch for exit signs. Being terminated should not come as a surprise, but it sometimes does. Some companies provide no warning to employees about to be terminated, for fear that advance notice may result in damage to the company—from sabotage of computer systems, for example. To be as prepared as possible, pay attention to your company's culture of termination (see the sidebar "Auf Wiedersehen: How to Fire Right"). Are people severed harshly and hustled out of the building, or is the door left open for a possible return? If the former, you may want to raise your guard and take some proactive steps. Likewise, watch for how the company itself is planning to exit, because your job depends on it. Examine the position and assignment changes within the company; do position descriptions or sets of responsibilities—including your own—imply an end? If yours does, it's entirely fair to ask whether your position will continue or how it will change once this particular work is complete. It's also helpful to cultivate a strong relationship with a founder or another trusted adviser who has "seen it all before"and who can help you stay aware of prospective changes. Remember—if you think you are about to be fired, you probably are. But if you are confused by signals being given to you, consider hiring an executive coach to help you sort them out (see the sidebar "Do You Need an Agent?").

Volunteer to be terminated. If the company's exit strategy appears to include you, consider volunteering to be terminated before it occurs. By initiating such a discussion, you become the actor rather than the one who is acted upon. Here's what happened when Joe, the CEO of a large firm, volunteered to be laid off as his company was acquired. The terms of his existing contract allowed Joe to stay on for two years as president of the newly merged organization while the CEO of the acquiring company became chairman. But rather than waiting to be terminated after the contract expired, Joe approached the new chairman with a suggestion. Joe said that while he knew that the contract was a fair one, he fully appreciated that the acquiring company would want to run things differently. He offered to resign, provided that an excellent severance agreement could be developed. The chairman, delighted to be saved the trouble of firing Joe, was extraordinarily generous, and Joe's severance package allowed him to retire altogether.

We do not mean to suggest that executives become overly wary and move from job to job or from company to company too quickly; a lot of mobility is as damaging as a little. Rather, we posit that in most cases, a degree of self-interest in one's career—as understood in its broadest, lifespanning sense—is both healthy and necessary. Executives who hold on to the tenure myth may find it difficult to assume an assignment mentality, and understandably so. It's natural to want to believe that the company for which you work so hard cares about you. But allowing yourself to be lulled into a false sense of security sets you up for shock and disappointment when you are fired or laid off.

On the corporate level, terminations are among the most predictable crises in business. When you develop an assignment mind-set, your termination becomes predictable on a personal level, too. Then even an experience as negative as being fired can turn out to be strangely empowering. It's ironic, but true: When you assume control over the way you are fired, you can gain control over your career.

Reprint R0107F
To order, see the next page
or call 800-988-0886 or 617-783-7500
or go to www.hbr.org

The insertion of a termination clause at the time of hire feels completely counterintuitive. Nevertheless, it's your best hedge against a bitter exit.

The Right Way to Be Fired

Further Reading

ARTICLES

Managing Oneself
by Peter F. Drucker
Harvard Business Review
March–April 1999
Product no. 4444

This article complements "The Right Way to Be Fired" by focusing on a powerful step in the career-management process: self-knowledge. As Drucker maintains, the old covenant that had corporations managing individuals' careers has given way to a work world in which employees must now navigate their own professional paths. Knowing how and when to change the work you do—and assessing which opportunities will provide the best fit for you—have never been more important. Drucker provides suggestions for determining 1) your most important strengths, 2) the ways in which you work best, 3) your values and desired work environment, and 4) the greatest contribution you can make in a new work situation. Armed with this information, you can identify—and execute—your best next move.

Job Sculpting: The Art of Retaining Your Best People
by Timothy Butler and James Waldroop
Harvard Business Review
September–October 1999
Product no. 4282

Butler and Waldroop take a closer look at what employees can do to manage their careers—and what managers can do to retain star performers. The authors describe a "job sculpting" strategy—matching employees to work that lets them express their deepest life interests. As the authors explain, many managers assume that a handsome paycheck is all they need to hang onto their best employees. But it's alignment between individuals' interests—e.g., conceptual thinking, counseling and mentoring, application of technology—and their job responsibilities that will keep employees loyal to your firm.

Butler and Waldroop describe techniques for helping employees identify their deepest interests—and then customizing jobs so employees can express those interests. Result? Talented workers committed to an effective career at your company.

A Market-Driven Approach to Retaining Talent
by Peter Cappelli
Harvard Business Review
January–February 2000
Product no. 6196

This article examines employee departures from the other side: that of managers who are losing their best workers in a free-for-all grab for talent. But as Cappelli explains, you don't keep your most valued employees by trying to hang onto everyone forever. Long-term, across-the-board employee retention simply isn't possible—or even desirable. After all, your firm may be a great place to work, but you can't always counter the pull of attractive opportunities and aggressive recruiters. The author recommends a different, innovative approach to retaining talent: Decide which employees you need to retain and for how long. Then influence who leaves and when, using customized programs. Cappelli describes powerful strategies for compensation, job design and customization, and hiring—as well as ways to adapt to the reality of attrition.

Harvard Business Review

To Order

For *Harvard Business Review* reprints and subscriptions, call 800-988-0886 or 617-783-7500. Go to www.hbr.org

For customized and quantity orders of *Harvard Business Review* article reprints, call 617-783-7626, or e-mail customizations@hbsp.harvard.edu

Harvard Business Review

www.hbr.org

Fulfillment doesn't come from clearing hurdles others set for you; it comes from clearing those you set for yourself.

Reaching Your Potential

by Robert S. Kaplan

Included with this full-text *Harvard Business Review* article:

Reprint R0807C

Reaching Your Potential

The Idea in Brief

Despite racking up impressive accomplishments, you feel frustrated with your career—convinced you should be achieving more. You may even wish you had chosen a different career altogether.

These feelings often stem from a common error: buying into others' definitions of success. To reach your potential, Kaplan suggests taking a deeply personal look at how *you* define success:

Begin by recognizing that managing your career is *your* responsibility. Then, follow these three steps:

- **Know yourself** by identifying your strengths and weaknesses and the activities you truly enjoy doing.

- **Excel** at the activities critical to success in your desired role.

- **Demonstrate character and leadership** by putting the interests of your company and colleagues ahead of your own.

The Idea in Practice

Kaplan offers these guidelines for reaching your potential at work:

KNOW YOURSELF

Write down your 2–3 greatest strengths *and* weaknesses. If (like most people) you struggle with identifying key weaknesses, solicit the views of people (peers, direct reports, trusted friends) who will tell you the brutal truth. Ask for very specific feedback ("How well do I listen?" "What is my leadership style?"). Be receptive to the input you receive.

Then figure out what you truly enjoy doing. What's your dream job? Resist the lure of a hot field: If you go into it without a strong enthusiasm for the actual work, you may waste a number of years before you admit it's the wrong job for you. Once you've chosen your ideal job, you'll have to start from scratch. But choosing a field you love gives you strength to weather the inevitable setbacks and long hours needed to reach your full potential in any career.

EXCEL AT CRITICAL ACTIVITIES

Identify the 3–4 activities essential for success in your desired or current role. Then develop a plan for excelling in these activities.

▶ Example:
A new division head at a large industrial company was struggling to grow sales and profits. Through interviews with staff and customers, he concluded that success in his business hinged on developing close relationships with top customers' purchasing managers, putting the right people in critical leadership positions, and staying at the cutting edge of product innovation. He began delegating activities less central to success so he could focus on raising the bar on the three success factors he had identified. Sales and profits improved.

DEMONSTRATE CHARACTER AND LEADERSHIP

Character and leadership make the difference between good and great performance. To demonstrate **character**:

- Put the interests of your company and colleagues ahead of your own, doing things for others without regard to what's in it for you.

- Adopt an owner's mindset, asking yourself what you would do if you were the ultimate decision maker.

- Be willing to make recommendations that will benefit your organization's overall performance, possibly to the detriment of your own unit. Trust that you'll eventually be rewarded.

To exhibit **leadership**, speak up—even when you're expressing an unpopular view. Your superiors desperately want dissenting opinions so they can make better choices. If you play it safe instead of asserting your heartfelt opinions, you may hit a plateau in your career.

Fulfillment doesn't come from clearing hurdles others set for you; it comes from clearing those you set for yourself.

MANAGING YOURSELF

Reaching Your Potential

by Robert S. Kaplan

Ambitious professionals often spend a substantial amount of time thinking about strategies that will help them achieve greater levels of success. They strive for a more impressive job title, higher compensation, and responsibility for more sizable revenues, profits, and numbers of employees. Their definitions of success are often heavily influenced by family, friends, and colleagues.

Yet many ultimately find that, despite their efforts and accomplishments, they lack a true sense of professional satisfaction and fulfillment. During my career with Goldman Sachs, as well as over the past few years of teaching and coaching managers and MBA students at Harvard Business School, I have met a surprisingly large number of impressive executives who expressed deep frustration with their careers. They looked back and felt that they should have achieved more or even wished that they had chosen a different career altogether.

Consider a very successful research analyst at a large securities firm who came to see me

because he was discouraged with his career progress. This was particularly ironic because he was well known, highly regarded (ranked number one in his industry sector), and well compensated. He told me that, after 10 years, he was tired of his job, disliked his boss, and felt he had no potential for further upward mobility. Most of all, he had always wanted to be an investment manager, but he had started out as an analyst and never really reassessed his career path. He felt trapped. He feared losing his stature and didn't want to let anyone down, but at the same time he didn't want to keep doing what he was doing.

As we talked, he wondered if he'd been so busy trying to reach specific milestones and impress other people that he'd lost sight of what he really enjoyed doing. The truth was that he loved analyzing stocks and assessing management teams, but he also wanted to have the responsibility for making the actual investment decisions and then be held accountable for the results. I encouraged him to take action and speak to a number of investment firms (including his current employer) about a career change. After doing this, he ultimately was offered and accepted a portfolio manager position in the asset management division of his current firm. He learned that his firm's leaders wanted to retain him regardless of job description and that they were quite surprised to find out he wanted to be on the investment side of the business. He has since become a superb investment manager, and although he wishes he'd stepped back and reexamined his career years earlier, he's thrilled that he made the switch while there was "still time."

If you are experiencing similar feelings of frustration or even regret about the direction of your career, this article is intended to help you examine the question, "Am I reaching my potential?" This is not the same as asking, "How do I rise to the top?" or "How can I be successful in my career?" Rather, it's about taking a very personal look at how *you* define success in your heart of hearts and then finding *your* path to get there.

To do that, you must step back and reassess your career—starting with the recognition that managing it is your responsibility. Too many people feel like victims in their careers, when in fact they have a substantial degree of control. Seizing control requires you to take a fresh look at your behavior in three main areas: knowing yourself, excelling at critical tasks, and demonstrating character and leadership.

Knowing Yourself

Taking responsibility for your career starts with an accurate assessment of your current skills and performance. Can you write down your two or three greatest strengths and your two or three most significant weaknesses? While most people can detail their strengths, they often struggle to identify key weaknesses. This exercise involves meaningful reflection and, almost always, requires soliciting the views of people who will tell you the brutal truth. Unfortunately, you often can't count on your boss to accurately assess your strengths or to be willing to confront you with what you're doing wrong. It's up to you to take control of this process by seeking coaching, asking for very specific feedback, and being receptive to input from a wide variety of people at various levels within your organization. This gather-

ing of feedback needs to be an ongoing process because, as your career progresses, you will face new challenges and demands.

Recently I met with a division head of a large professional services firm. Though he'd been a rising star for several years, he felt he'd begun to stagnate. His direct reports and his CEO no longer seemed engaged and enthusiastic in their dealings with him, and he didn't know why. In our discussions, he was able to specifically describe his strengths, but when I asked about his weaknesses, he gave me fairly generic responses, such as "Maybe I'm too impatient" and "I need to raise my profile." When I pressed him about feedback from his boss he still struggled to identify even one specific weakness. I sent him off on an assignment: Interview at least five colleagues and subordinates.

He returned a few weeks later with several "surprises." He'd heard, for example, that while he was detail-oriented and decisive, he micromanaged, had a dictatorial style, and failed to listen. Armed with these insights, he sought coaching, started working on his flaws, and began regularly soliciting feedback from his colleagues and subordinates. A year later he reported that his effectiveness had improved as a result of these ongoing efforts, and he was once again feeling confident and optimistic about his career.

This type of initiative takes time, humility, and a willingness to confront weaknesses, fears, and blind spots that many of us would rather ignore. But I never cease to be impressed by the capacity of people to change and improve once they recognize their shortcomings as well as their strengths.

Of course, getting others to tell you where you're falling short isn't easy—particularly if they're your subordinates. It must be done in one-on-one conversations, and you need to give potential coaches time to learn that you're sincere. When your employees see you actually act on their feedback, they are likely to become more proactive in offering advice, because they know you value their input. Your subordinates and colleagues will also feel they have a stake in your success and that of your unit—which will make them more likely to enjoy working with you.

Once you have a grip on your strengths and weaknesses, your next challenge is to figure out what you truly enjoy doing. What's your

Robert S. Kaplan (rokaplan@hbs.edu) is the acting president and CEO of Harvard Management Company and a professor of management practice at Harvard Business School in Boston. He is also a former vice chairman of the Goldman Sachs Group.

dream job? How well does it match what you currently do? Many people either don't know what their passions are or are so focused on the views of their peers that they drift into the wrong career. I was recently approached by an MBA student who wanted advice on whether to go work for a hedge fund, a private equity firm, or an investment bank. When asked whether he had an interest in financial markets, he quickly said no. He wasn't even sure about the key tasks that each of those jobs would entail. When asked what he would do if he had $10 million in the bank, however, his answer was very clear: pursue a career in the music industry. He was a concert-level musician and loved the music business. Once he recognized how much he had been swayed by his fellow students' bias toward the lucrative financial services industry, he realized he needed to rethink his choices.

The conventional wisdom about the attractiveness of various careers changes constantly. Twenty-five years ago the medical and legal professions were considered financially rewarding and socially desirable. Today, a number of doctors and lawyers are frustrated in their jobs and realize that they might have based their career choices excessively on the views of their peers and popular opinion, instead of on whether they would actually love the work. Hedge funds and private equity are today's hot fields, but people who go into them without a strong enthusiasm for the actual tasks may find themselves starting from scratch a few years down the line. Loving what you do gives you the strength to weather personal setbacks, overcome adversity, face and address your weaknesses, and work the long hours typically needed to reach your full potential.

Excelling at Critical Tasks

It's very difficult to succeed if you don't excel at the tasks that are central to your chosen enterprise. That sounds painfully simple, but many executives fail to identify the three or four most important activities that lead to success in their job or business. If you're a medical researcher, the three keys are likely to be conducting cutting-edge research, getting published, and fund-raising. If you manage a large sales force, the crucial tasks might be attracting, retaining, and developing outstanding salespeople; customer segmentation; and client relationship management. If you're assessing a potential job move, you need to know what will drive success in the new position and, then, ask yourself whether you enjoy those key tasks. In your current job, identifying critical tasks helps you determine how to spend your time and develop your skills.

Promising leaders sometimes lose sight of this connection. Not long ago, a new division head at a large industrial company told me that he was struggling to grow sales and profits. He complained that he was spending too much time fighting fires and didn't have enough hours in the day. When I asked him to identify the three main drivers of success in his business, he realized that he wasn't sure. He spent the next several weeks interviewing staff and customers, and concluded that success in his business depended on developing close relationships with the purchasing managers at each of his top 25 customers, putting the right people in critical sales and manufacturing leadership positions, and staying at the cutting edge of product innovation. He also realized that his division was performing poorly in all three areas.

He proceeded to clear his calendar, force himself to delegate tasks that were less central to success, and focus on raising the bar in each of these areas. Six months later he reported that he had replaced a number of executives—

Career Counsel: Follow Your Own Path

Reaching your potential requires introspection and certain proactive behaviors—but it starts with a basic philosophy, or "rules of the road."

1. Managing your career is 100% your responsibility, and you need to act accordingly. Many promising professionals expect their superiors to mentor them, give them thoughtful coaching, provide them with challenging opportunities, and generally steer their development. Such a passive approach is likely to derail you at some point. While your superiors will play a role, your career is your own.

2. Be wary of conventional wisdom. It's almost always wrong—for you. Hopping on the bandwagon may feel good initially but often leads to painful regrets years later. To reach your potential, you must filter out peer pressure and popular opinion; assess your own passions, skills, and convictions; and then be courageous enough to act on them.

3. Have faith that, although justice may not prevail at any given point in time, it should generally prevail over time. When you do suffer an injustice, you need to be willing to step back and objectively assess your own role in these events. That mind-set will help you learn from inevitable setbacks and eventually bounce back. It will also help you stay focused on issues you can control as well as bolster your determination to act like the ultimate decision maker.

I have seen many people stall their careers by playing it safe.

including the sales manager and head of product development—and created an executive committee that met weekly to discuss critical business issues. He also reported that he'd become much more disciplined in matching his priorities (and those of his leadership team) with the keys to success for the business. Sales and profits began to improve, and he felt confident that he would resume his upward career trajectory.

Demonstrating Character and Leadership

While seemingly amorphous, character and leadership often make the difference between good performance and great performance. One measure of character is the degree to which you put the interests of your company and colleagues ahead of your own. Excellent leaders are willing to do things for others without regard to what's in it for them. They coach and mentor. They have the mindset of an owner and figure out what they would do if they were the ultimate decision maker. They're willing to make a recommendation that would benefit the organization's overall performance, possibly to the detriment of their own unit. They have the courage to trust that they will eventually be rewarded, even if their actions may not be in their own short-term interest.

Being a leader also means being willing to speak up, even when you're expressing an unpopular view. CEOs' proposals often generate head nodding, even from people who secretly harbor serious reservations. In reality, most chief executives desperately want dissenting opinions so they can make better choices. While emerging leaders must use good judgment regarding the tone and timing of their dissent, they also need to be aware that they can hit a plateau by playing it safe when they should be asserting their heartfelt opinions.

One CEO recounted to me his regrets over a recent key hire. His top three reports had each interviewed the various job candidates and expressed no major concerns about the final choice. After the new hire was on board—and had begun to struggle—it came to light that two of the three senior managers had privately held significant reservations but concluded that the CEO's mind was made up and that speaking out was unwise. The CEO was furious. Though he recognized his own role in the

mess (he vowed to more actively encourage dissent), he also lowered his opinion of the two executives who failed to express their views.

Otherwise confident executives sometimes overestimate the career risk of speaking up and meaningfully underestimate the risk of staying silent. I encourage people to develop various approaches to help them overcome this hesitancy: For example, I've counseled emerging executives to save their money to build financial security and to avoid getting too emotionally attached to their jobs. Though it may seem that you'll never find another great job, you have to have faith that there are many attractive opportunities outside your firm.

In some cases, I advise people to become experts in some specific business area in order to build their confidence. I also encourage people to spend more time deciding what they truly believe versus trying to guess what the boss might want to hear. At work, as in competitive sports, you must play with confidence and even a little abandon. I've talked to several executives whose finest moments came when they gathered their courage and confidently expressed disagreement with their boss and peers. To their surprise, they found that they were treated with more respect after these episodes.

Most outstanding CEOs value emerging executives who assert themselves out of genuine concern for what is best for the company. Doing the right thing is a reward in itself—psychologically in the short run and professionally in the longer run. Of course, this approach requires that you have some reasonable level of faith that justice will prevail. I have seldom seen people hurt their careers by speaking up and appropriately articulating a well-thought-out contrary position (even when it was unpopular). However, I have seen many bitter and confused people who stalled their careers by playing it safe.

• • •

Every rewarding career will bring ups and downs, bad days, bad weeks, and bad months. Everyone will face setbacks and discouraging situations. Some people abandon their plans when they hit one of these bumps. They lose their way and ultimately undermine their own performance—and the wound is all the more painful because it is self-inflicted. The advice in this article is intended to help you avoid such self-inflicted wounds. There's nothing anyone can do to prevent you from reaching your potential; the challenge is for you to identify your dream, develop the skills to get there, and exhibit character and leadership. Then, you need to have the courage to periodically reassess, make adjustments, and pursue a course that reflects who you truly are.

Reprint R0807C
To order, see the next page
or call 800-988-0886 or 617-783-7500
or go to www.hbr.org

Reaching Your Potential

Further Reading

ARTICLE
What to Ask the Person in the Mirror
by Robert S. Kaplan
Harvard Business Review
January 2007
Product no. R0701H

In this earlier article, Kaplan highlights the importance of knowing yourself to reaching your potential as a leader. As you climb the corporate ladder, it becomes harder to get candid feedback on your strengths and weaknesses, so you risk making mistakes that damage your organization and your reputation. To stay on your game, regularly ask yourself questions related to key leadership challenges. For example, "Am I communicating a vision for my business to my employees?" "Am I spending my time in ways that enable me to achieve my priorities?" "Do I give people timely and direct feedback they can act on?" "How do I behave under pressure?"

COLLECTION
Managing Yourself, 2nd Edition
by Tony Schwartz, Catherine McCarthy, Stewart D. Friedman, Donald N. Sull, Dominic Houlder, and Peter F. Drucker
HBR Article Collection
April 2008
Product no. 10097

This collection offers strategies for changing course if you feel dissatisfied with your life's direction:

- If you're putting in longer hours, only to become less productive and more exhausted, read the suggestions for reviving four types of personal energy in "Manage Your Energy, Not Your Time," by Tony Schwartz and Catherine McCarthy. For example, replenish emotional energy by viewing upsetting situations as learning opportunities. Free up physical energy by setting an earlier bedtime and reducing alcohol intake.

- If you're making trade-offs between your professional and personal obligations, consider making small changes that benefit multiple dimensions of your life, as Stewart Friedman recommends in "Be a Better Leader, Have a Richer Life." For instance, join a club with coworkers. You'll forge closer friendships with them, strengthening your sense of community and improving on-the-job collaboration.

- If you've lost touch with what matters most to you, explore "Do Your Commitments Match Your Convictions?" by Donald N. Sull and Dominic Houlder. They recommend a disciplined process for articulating your deepest values, determining which are receiving insufficient time and energy from you, and closing gaps.

- If you want to know your strengths, weaknesses, and desired work environment better, read Peter F. Drucker's "Managing Yourself." He presents a way to clarify five aspects of your professional identity and recommends seeking job opportunities and environments that fit that identity most closely.

Harvard Business Review ⚞

To Order

For *Harvard Business Review* reprints and subscriptions, call 800-988-0886 or 617-783-7500. Go to www.hbr.org

For customized and quantity orders of *Harvard Business Review* article reprints, call 617-783-7626, or e-mail customizations@hbsp.harvard.edu

www.hbrreprints.org

The science of stamina has advanced to the point where individuals, teams, and whole organizations can, with some straightforward interventions, significantly increase their capacity to get things done.

MANAGING YOURSELF

Manage Your Energy, Not Your Time

by Tony Schwartz and Catherine McCarthy

Included with this full-text *Harvard Business Review* article:

Manage Your Energy, Not Your Time

The Idea in Brief

Organizations are demanding ever-higher performance from their workforces. People are trying to comply, but the usual method—putting in longer hours—has backfired. They're getting exhausted, disengaged, and sick. And they're defecting to healthier job environments.

Longer days at the office don't work because time is a limited resource. But personal energy is renewable, say Schwartz and McCarthy. By fostering deceptively simple **rituals** that help employees regularly replenish their energy, organizations build workers' physical, emotional, and mental resilience. These rituals include taking brief breaks at specific intervals, expressing appreciation to others, reducing interruptions, and spending more time on activities people do best and enjoy most.

Help your employees systematically rejuvenate their personal energy, and the benefits go straight to your bottom line. Take Wachovia Bank: Participants in an energy renewal program produced 13 percentage points greater year-over-year in revenues from loans than a control group did. And they exceeded the control group's gains in revenues from deposits by 20 percentage points.

The Idea in Practice

Schwartz and McCarthy recommend these practices for renewing four dimensions of personal energy:

PHYSICAL ENERGY

- Enhance your sleep by setting an earlier bedtime and reducing alcohol use.

- Reduce stress by engaging in cardiovascular activity at least three times a week and strength training at least once.

- Eat small meals and light snacks every three hours.

- Learn to notice signs of imminent energy flagging, including restlessness, yawning, hunger, and difficulty concentrating.

- Take brief but regular breaks, away from your desk, at 90- to 120-minute intervals throughout the day.

EMOTIONAL ENERGY

- Defuse negative emotions—irritability, impatience, anxiety, insecurity—through deep abdominal breathing.

- Fuel positive emotions in yourself and others by regularly expressing appreciation to others in detailed, specific terms through notes, e-mails, calls, or conversations.

- Look at upsetting situations through new lenses. Adopt a "reverse lens" to ask, "What would the other person in this conflict say, and how might he be right?" Use a "long lens" to ask, "How will I likely view this situation in six months?" Employ a "wide lens" to ask, "How can I grow and learn from this situation?"

MENTAL ENERGY

- Reduce interruptions by performing high-concentration tasks away from phones and e-mail.

- Respond to voice mails and e-mails at designated times during the day.

- Every night, identify the most important challenge for the next day. Then make it your first priority when you arrive at work in the morning.

SPIRITUAL ENERGY

- Identify your "sweet spot" activities—those that give you feelings of effectiveness, effortless absorption, and fulfillment. Find ways to do more of these. One executive who hated doing sales reports delegated them to someone who loved that activity.

- Allocate time and energy to what you consider most important. For example, spend the last 20 minutes of your evening commute relaxing, so you can connect with your family once you're home.

- Live your core values. For instance, if consideration is important to you but you're perpetually late for meetings, practice intentionally showing up five minutes early for meetings.

HOW COMPANIES CAN HELP

To support energy renewal rituals in your firm:

- Build "renewal rooms" where people can go to relax and refuel.

- Subsidize gym memberships.

- Encourage managers to gather employees for midday workouts.

- Suggest that people stop checking e-mails during meetings.

The science of stamina has advanced to the point where individuals, teams, and whole organizations can, with some straightforward interventions, significantly increase their capacity to get things done.

Manage Your Energy, Not Your Time

by Tony Schwartz and Catherine McCarthy

Steve Wanner is a highly respected 37-year-old partner at Ernst & Young, married with four young children. When we met him a year ago, he was working 12- to 14-hour days, felt perpetually exhausted, and found it difficult to fully engage with his family in the evenings, which left him feeling guilty and dissatisfied. He slept poorly, made no time to exercise, and seldom ate healthy meals, instead grabbing a bite to eat on the run or while working at his desk.

Wanner's experience is not uncommon. Most of us respond to rising demands in the workplace by putting in longer hours, which inevitably take a toll on us physically, mentally, and emotionally. That leads to declining levels of engagement, increasing levels of distraction, high turnover rates, and soaring medical costs among employees. We at the Energy Project have worked with thousands of leaders and managers in the course of doing consulting and coaching at large organizations during the past five years. With remarkable consistency, these executives tell us they're pushing themselves harder than ever

to keep up and increasingly feel they are at a breaking point.

The core problem with working longer hours is that time is a finite resource. Energy is a different story. Defined in physics as the capacity to work, energy comes from four main wellsprings in human beings: the body, emotions, mind, and spirit. In each, energy can be systematically expanded and regularly renewed by establishing specific rituals—behaviors that are intentionally practiced and precisely scheduled, with the goal of making them unconscious and automatic as quickly as possible.

To effectively reenergize their workforces, organizations need to shift their emphasis from getting more out of people to investing more in them, so they are motivated—and able—to bring more of themselves to work every day. To recharge themselves, individuals need to recognize the costs of energy-depleting behaviors and then take responsibility for changing them, regardless of the circumstances they're facing.

The rituals and behaviors Wanner established to better manage his energy transformed his life. He set an earlier bedtime and gave up drinking, which had disrupted his sleep. As a consequence, when he woke up he felt more rested and more motivated to exercise, which he now does almost every morning. In less than two months he lost 15 pounds. After working out he now sits down with his family for breakfast. Wanner still puts in long hours on the job, but he renews himself regularly along the way. He leaves his desk for lunch and usually takes a morning and an afternoon walk outside. When he arrives at home in the evening, he's more relaxed and better able to connect with his wife and children.

Establishing simple rituals like these can lead to striking results across organizations. At Wachovia Bank, we took a group of employees through a pilot energy management program and then measured their performance against that of a control group. The participants outperformed the controls on a series of financial metrics, such as the value of loans they generated. They also reported substantial improvements in their customer relationships, their engagement with work, and their personal satisfaction. In this article, we'll describe the Wachovia study in a little more detail. Then we'll explain what executives and managers can do to increase and regularly renew work capacity—the approach used by the Energy Project, which builds on, deepens, and extends several core concepts developed by Tony's former partner Jim Loehr in his seminal work with athletes.

Linking Capacity and Performance at Wachovia

Most large organizations invest in developing employees' skills, knowledge, and competence. Very few help build and sustain their capacity—their energy—which is typically taken for granted. In fact, greater capacity makes it possible to get more done in less time at a higher level of engagement and with more sustainability. Our experience at Wachovia bore this out.

In early 2006 we took 106 employees at 12 regional banks in southern New Jersey through a curriculum of four modules, each of which focused on specific strategies for strengthening one of the four main dimen-

sions of energy. We delivered it at one-month intervals to groups of approximately 20 to 25, ranging from senior leaders to lower-level managers. We also assigned each attendee a fellow employee as a source of support between sessions. Using Wachovia's own key performance metrics, we evaluated how the participant group performed compared with a group of employees at similar levels at a nearby set of Wachovia banks who did not go through the training. To create a credible basis for comparison, we looked at year-over-year percentage changes in performance across several metrics.

On a measure called the "Big 3"—revenues from three kinds of loans—the participants showed a year-over-year increase that was 13 percentage points greater than the control group's in the first three months of our study. On revenues from deposits, the participants exceeded the control group's year-over-year gain by 20 percentage points during that same period. The precise gains varied month by month, but with only a handful of exceptions, the participants continued to significantly outperform the control group for a full year after completing the program. Although other variables undoubtedly influenced these outcomes, the participants' superior performance was notable in its consistency. (See the exhibit "How Energy Renewal Programs Boosted Productivity at Wachovia.")

We also asked participants how the program influenced them personally. Sixty-eight percent reported that it had a positive impact on their relationships with clients and customers. Seventy-one percent said that it had a noticeable or substantial positive impact on their productivity and performance. These findings corroborated a raft of anecdotal evidence we've gathered about the effectiveness of this approach among leaders at other large companies such as Ernst & Young, Sony, Deutsche Bank, Nokia, ING Direct, Ford, and MasterCard.

The Body: Physical Energy

Our program begins by focusing on physical energy. It is scarcely news that inadequate nutrition, exercise, sleep, and rest diminish people's basic energy levels, as well as their ability to manage their emotions and focus their attention. Nonetheless, many executives don't find ways to practice consistently

Tony Schwartz (tony@theenergyproject .com) is the president and founder of the Energy Project in New York City, and a coauthor of *The Power of Full Engagement: Managing Energy, Not Time, Is the Key to High Performance and Personal Renewal* (Free Press, 2003).
Catherine McCarthy (catherine@ theenergyproject.com) is a senior vice president at the Energy Project.

healthy behaviors, given all the other demands in their lives.

Before participants in our program begin to explore ways to increase their physical energy, they take an energy audit, which includes four questions in each energy dimension—body, emotions, mind, and spirit. (See the exhibit "Are You Headed for an Energy Crisis?") On average, participants get eight to ten of those 16 questions "wrong," meaning they're doing things such as skipping breakfast, failing to express appreciation to others, struggling to focus on one thing at a time, or spending too little time on activities that give them a sense of purpose. While most participants aren't surprised to learn these behaviors are counterproductive, having them all listed in one place is often uncomfortable, sobering, and galvanizing. The audit highlights employees' greatest energy deficits. Participants also fill out charts designed to raise their awareness about how their exercise, diet, and sleep practices influence their energy levels.

The next step is to identify rituals for building and renewing physical energy. When Gary Faro, a vice president at Wachovia, began the program, he was significantly overweight, ate poorly, lacked a regular exercise routine, worked long hours, and typically slept no more than five or six hours a night. That is not an unusual profile among the leaders and managers we see. Over the course of the program, Faro began regular cardiovascular and strength training. He started going to bed at a designated time and sleeping longer. He changed his eating habits from two big meals a day ("Where I usually gorged myself," he says) to smaller meals and light snacks every three hours. The aim was to help him stabilize his glucose levels over the course of the day, avoiding peaks and valleys. He lost 50 pounds in the process, and his energy levels soared. "I used to schedule tough projects for the morning, when I knew that I would be more focused," Faro says. "I don't have to do that anymore because I find that I'm just as focused now at 5 PM as I am at 8 AM."

Another key ritual Faro adopted was to take brief but regular breaks at specific intervals throughout the workday—always leaving his desk. The value of such breaks is grounded in our physiology. "Ultradian rhythms" refer to 90- to 120-minute cycles during which our bodies slowly move from a high-energy state into a physiological trough. Toward the end of each cycle, the body begins to crave a period of recovery. The signals include physical restlessness, yawning, hunger, and difficulty concentrating, but many of us ignore them and keep working. The consequence is that our energy reservoir—our remaining capacity—burns down as the day wears on.

Intermittent breaks for renewal, we have found, result in higher and more sustainable performance. The length of renewal is less important than the quality. It is possible to get a great deal of recovery in a short time—as little as several minutes—if it involves a ritual that allows you to disengage from work and truly change channels. That could range from getting up to talk to a colleague about something other than work, to listening to music on an iPod, to walking up and down stairs in an office building. While breaks are countercultural in most organizations and counterintuitive for many high achievers, their value is multifaceted.

Matthew Lang is a managing director for Sony in South Africa. He adopted some of the same rituals that Faro did, including a

How Energy Renewal Programs Boosted Productivity at Wachovia

At Wachovia Bank, employees participating in an energy renewal program outperformed a control group of employees, demonstrating significantly greater improvements in year-over-year performance during the first quarter of 2006.

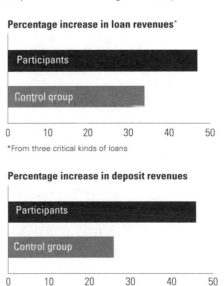

Percentage increase in loan revenues*

Participants

Control group

0   10   20   30   40   50

*From three critical kinds of loans

Percentage increase in deposit revenues

Participants

Control group

0   10   20   30   40   50

20-minute walk in the afternoons. Lang's walk not only gives him a mental and emotional breather and some exercise but also has become the time when he gets his best creative ideas. That's because when he walks he is not actively thinking, which allows the dominant left hemisphere of his brain to give way to the right hemisphere with its greater capacity to see the big picture and make imaginative leaps.

The Emotions: Quality of Energy

When people are able to take more control of their emotions, they can improve the quality of their energy, regardless of the external pressures they're facing. To do this, they first must become more aware of how they feel at various points during the workday and of the impact these emotions have on their effectiveness. Most people realize that they tend to perform best when they're feeling positive energy. What they find surprising is that they're not able to perform well or to lead effectively when they're feeling any other way.

Unfortunately, without intermittent recovery, we're not physiologically capable of sustaining highly positive emotions for long periods. Confronted with relentless demands and unexpected challenges, people tend to slip into negative emotions—the fight-or-flight mode—often multiple times in a day. They become irritable and impatient, or anxious and insecure. Such states of mind drain people's energy and cause friction in their relationships. Fight-or-flight emotions also make it impossible to think clearly, logically, and reflectively. When executives learn to recognize what kinds of events trigger their negative emotions, they gain greater capacity to take control of their reactions.

One simple but powerful ritual for defusing negative emotions is what we call "buying time." Deep abdominal breathing is one way to do that. Exhaling slowly for five or six seconds induces relaxation and recovery, and turns off the fight-or-flight response. When we began working with Fujio Nishida, president of Sony Europe, he had a habit of lighting up

Are You Headed for an Energy Crisis?

Please check the statements below that are true for you.

Body

__ I don't regularly get at least seven to eight hours of sleep, and I often wake up feeling tired.

__ I frequently skip breakfast, or I settle for something that isn't nutritious.

__ I don't work out enough (meaning cardiovascular training at least three times a week and strength training at least once a week).

__ I don't take regular breaks during the day to truly renew and recharge, or I often eat lunch at my desk, if I eat it at all.

Emotions

__ I frequently find myself feeling irritable, impatient, or anxious at work, especially when work is demanding.

__ I don't have enough time with my family and loved ones, and when I'm with them, I'm not always really with them.

__ I have too little time for the activities that I most deeply enjoy.

__ I don't stop frequently enough to express

my appreciation to others or to savor my accomplishments and blessings.

Mind

__ I have difficulty focusing on one thing at a time, and I am easily distracted during the day, especially by e-mail.

__ I spend much of my day reacting to immediate crises and demands rather than focusing on activities with longer-term value and high leverage.

__ I don't take enough time for reflection, strategizing, and creative thinking.

__ I work in the evenings or on weekends, and I almost never take an e-mail–free vacation.

Spirit

__ I don't spend enough time at work doing what I do best and enjoy most.

__ There are significant gaps between what I say is most important to me in my life and how I actually allocate my time and energy.

__ My decisions at work are more often influenced by external demands than by a strong, clear sense of my own purpose.

__ I don't invest enough time and energy in

making a positive difference to others or to the world.

• • •

How is your overall energy?
Total number of statements checked: __

Guide to scores

0–3: Excellent energy management skills

4–6: Reasonable energy management skills

7–10: Significant energy management deficits

11–16: A full-fledged energy management crisis

What do you need to work on?

Number of checks in each category:

Body __

Mind __

Emotions __

Spirit __

Guide to category scores

0: Excellent energy management skills

1: Strong energy management skills

2: Significant deficits

3: Poor energy management skills

4: A full-fledged energy crisis

a cigarette each time something especially stressful occurred—at least two or three times a day. Otherwise, he didn't smoke. We taught him the breathing exercise as an alternative, and it worked immediately: Nishida found he no longer had the desire for a cigarette. It wasn't the smoking that had given him relief from the stress, we concluded, but the relaxation prompted by the deep inhalation and exhalation.

A powerful ritual that fuels positive emotions is expressing appreciation to others, a practice that seems to be as beneficial to the giver as to the receiver. It can take the form of a handwritten note, an e-mail, a call, or a conversation—and the more detailed and specific, the higher the impact. As with all rituals, setting aside a particular time to do it vastly increases the chances of success. Ben Jenkins, vice chairman and president of the General Bank at Wachovia in Charlotte, North Carolina, built his appreciation ritual into time set aside for mentoring. He began scheduling lunches or dinners regularly with people who worked for him. Previously, the only sit-downs he'd had with his direct reports were to hear monthly reports on their numbers or to give them yearly performance reviews. Now, over meals, he makes it a priority to recognize their accomplishments and also to talk with them about their lives and their aspirations rather than their immediate work responsibilities.

Finally, people can cultivate positive emotions by learning to change the stories they tell themselves about the events in their lives. Often, people in conflict cast themselves in the role of victim, blaming others or external circumstances for their problems. Becoming aware of the difference between the facts in a given situation and the way we interpret those facts can be powerful in itself. It's been a revelation for many of the people we work with to discover they have a choice about how to view a given event and to recognize how powerfully the story they tell influences the emotions they feel. We teach them to tell the most hopeful and personally empowering story possible in any given situation, without denying or minimizing the facts.

The most effective way people can change a story is to view it through any of three new lenses, which are all alternatives to seeing the world from the victim perspective. With the

reverse lens, for example, people ask themselves, "What would the other person in this conflict say and in what ways might that be true?" With the *long lens* they ask, "How will I most likely view this situation in six months?" With the *wide lens* they ask themselves, "Regardless of the outcome of this issue, how can I grow and learn from it?" Each of these lenses can help people intentionally cultivate more positive emotions.

Nicolas Babin, director of corporate communications for Sony Europe, was the point person for calls from reporters when Sony went through several recalls of its batteries in 2006. Over time he found his work increasingly exhausting and dispiriting. After practicing the lens exercises, he began finding ways to tell himself a more positive and empowering story about his role. "I realized," he explains, "that this was an opportunity for me to build stronger relationships with journalists by being accessible to them and to increase Sony's credibility by being straightforward and honest."

The Mind: Focus of Energy

Many executives view multitasking as a necessity in the face of all the demands they juggle, but it actually undermines productivity. Distractions are costly: A temporary shift in attention from one task to another—stopping to answer an e-mail or take a phone call, for instance—increases the amount of time necessary to finish the primary task by as much as 25%, a phenomenon known as "switching time." It's far more efficient to fully focus for 90 to 120 minutes, take a true break, and then fully focus on the next activity. We refer to these work periods as "ultradian sprints."

Once people see how much they struggle to concentrate, they can create rituals to reduce the relentless interruptions that technology has introduced in their lives. We start out with an exercise that forces them to face the impact of daily distractions. They attempt to complete a complex task and are regularly interrupted—an experience that, people report, ends up feeling much like everyday life.

Dan Cluna, a vice president at Wachovia, designed two rituals to better focus his attention. The first one is to leave his desk and go into a conference room, away from phones and e-mail, whenever he has a task that requires concentration. He now finishes reports

People can cultivate positive energy by learning to change the stories they tell themselves about the events in their lives. We teach them to tell the most hopeful stories possible.

in a third of the time they used to require. Cluna built his second ritual around meetings at branches with the financial specialists who report to him. Previously, he would answer his phone whenever it rang during these meetings. As a consequence, the meetings he scheduled for an hour often stretched to two, and he rarely gave anyone his full attention. Now Cluna lets his phone go to voice mail, so that he can focus completely on the person in front of him. He now answers the accumulated voice-mail messages when he has downtime between meetings.

E&Y's hard-charging Wanner used to answer e-mail constantly throughout the day—whenever he heard a "ping." Then he created a ritual of checking his e-mail just twice a day—at 10:15 AM and 2:30 PM. Whereas previously he couldn't keep up with all his messages, he discovered he could clear his in-box each time he opened it—the reward of fully focusing his attention on e-mail for 45 minutes at a time. Wanner has also reset the expectations of all the people he regularly communicates with by e-mail. "I've told them if it's an emergency and they need an instant response, they can call me and I'll always pick up," he says. Nine months later he has yet to receive such a call.

Michael Henke, a senior manager at E&Y, sat his team down at the start of the busy season last winter and told them that at certain points during the day he was going to turn off his Sametime (an in-house instant-message system). The result, he said, was that he would be less available to them for questions. Like Wanner, he told his team to call him if any emergency arose, but they rarely did. He also encouraged the group to take regular breaks throughout the day and to eat more regularly. They finished the busy season under budget and more profitable than other teams that hadn't followed the energy renewal program. "We got the same amount of work done in less time," says Henke. "It made for a win-win."

Another way to mobilize mental energy is to focus systematically on activities that have the most long-term leverage. Unless people intentionally schedule time for more challenging work, they tend not to get to it at all or rush through it at the last minute. Perhaps the most effective focus ritual the executives we work with have adopted is to identify each

night the most important challenge for the next day and make it their very first priority when they arrive in the morning. Jean Luc Duquesne, a vice president for Sony Europe in Paris, used to answer his e-mail as soon as he got to the office, just as many people do. He now tries to concentrate the first hour of every day on the most important topic. He finds that he often emerges at 10 AM feeling as if he's already had a productive day.

The Human Spirit: Energy of Meaning and Purpose

People tap into the energy of the human spirit when their everyday work and activities are consistent with what they value most and with what gives them a sense of meaning and purpose. If the work they're doing really matters to them, they typically feel more positive energy, focus better, and demonstrate greater perseverance. Regrettably, the high demands and fast pace of corporate life don't leave much time to pay attention to these issues, and many people don't even recognize meaning and purpose as potential sources of energy. Indeed, if we tried to begin our program by focusing on the human spirit, it would likely have minimal impact. Only when participants have experienced the value of the rituals they establish in the other dimensions do they start to see that being attentive to their own deeper needs dramatically influences their effectiveness and satisfaction at work.

For E&Y partner Jonathan Anspacher, simply having the opportunity to ask himself a series of questions about what really mattered to him was both illuminating and energizing. "I think it's important to be a little introspective and say, 'What do you want to be remembered for?'" he told us. "You don't want to be remembered as the crazy partner who worked these long hours and had his people be miserable. When my kids call me and ask, 'Can you come to my band concert?' I want to say, 'Yes, I'll be there and I'll be in the front row.' I don't want to be the father that comes in and sits in the back and is on his Blackberry and has to step out to take a phone call."

To access the energy of the human spirit, people need to clarify priorities and establish accompanying rituals in three categories: doing what they do best and enjoy most at work; consciously allocating time and energy to the areas of their lives—work, family, health, service to others—they deem most important; and living their core values in their daily behaviors.

When you're attempting to discover what you do best and what you enjoy most, it's important to realize that these two things aren't necessarily mutually inclusive. You may get lots of positive feedback about something you're very good at but not truly enjoy it. Conversely, you can love doing something but have no gift for it, so that achieving success requires much more energy than it makes sense to invest.

To help program participants discover their areas of strength, we ask them to recall at least two work experiences in the past several months during which they found themselves in their "sweet spot"—feeling effective, effortlessly absorbed, inspired, and fulfilled. Then we have them deconstruct those experiences to understand precisely what energized them so positively and what specific talents they were drawing on. If leading strategy feels like a sweet spot, for example, is it being in charge that's most invigorating or participating in a creative endeavor? Or is it using a skill that comes to you easily and so feels good to exercise? Finally, we have people establish a ritual that will encourage them to do more of exactly that kind of activity at work.

A senior leader we worked with realized that one of the activities he least liked was reading and summarizing detailed sales reports, whereas one of his favorites was brainstorming new strategies. The leader found a direct report who loved immersing himself in numbers and delegated the sales report task to him—happily settling for brief oral summaries from him each day. The leader also began scheduling a free-form 90-minute strategy session every other week with the most creative people in his group.

In the second category, devoting time and energy to what's important to you, there is often a similar divide between what people say is important and what they actually do. Rituals can help close this gap. When Jean Luc Duquesne, the Sony Europe vice president, thought hard about his personal priorities, he realized that spending time with his family was what mattered most to him, but it often got squeezed out of his day. So he instituted a ritual in which he switches off for at least three hours every evening when he gets home, so he can focus on his family. "I'm still not an expert on PlayStation," he told us, "but according to my youngest son, I'm learning and I'm a good student." Steve Wanner, who used to talk on the cell phone all the way to his front door on his commute home, has chosen a specific spot 20 minutes from his house where he ends whatever call he's on and puts away the phone. He spends the rest of his commute relaxing so that when he does arrive home, he's less preoccupied with work and more available to his wife and children.

The third category, practicing your core values in your everyday behavior, is a challenge for many as well. Most people are living at such a furious pace that they rarely stop to ask themselves what they stand for and who they want to be. As a consequence, they let external demands dictate their actions.

We don't suggest that people explicitly define their values, because the results are usually too predictable. Instead, we seek to uncover them, in part by asking questions that are inadvertently revealing, such as, "What are the qualities that you find most off-putting when you see them in others?" By describing what they can't stand, people unintentionally divulge what they stand for. If you are very offended by stinginess, for example, generosity is probably one of your key values. If you are especially put off by rudeness in others, it's likely that consideration is a high value for you. As in the other categories, establishing rituals can help bridge the gap between the values you aspire to and how you currently behave. If you discover that consideration is a key value, but you are perpetually late for meetings, the ritual might be to end the meetings you run five minutes earlier than usual and intentionally show up five minutes early for the meeting that follows.

Addressing these three categories helps people go a long way toward achieving a greater sense of alignment, satisfaction, and well-being in their lives on and off the job. Those feelings are a source of positive energy in their own right and reinforce people's desire to persist at rituals in other energy dimensions as well.

• • •

This new way of working takes hold only to the degree that organizations support their people in adopting new behaviors. We have learned, sometimes painfully, that not all executives and companies are prepared to embrace the notion that personal renewal for employees will lead to better and more sustainable performance. To succeed, renewal efforts need solid support and commitment from senior management, beginning with the key decision maker.

At Wachovia, Susanne Svizeny, the president of the region in which we conducted our study, was the primary cheerleader for the program. She embraced the principles in her own life and made a series of personal changes, including a visible commitment to building more regular renewal rituals into her work life. Next, she took it upon herself to foster the excitement and commitment of her leadership team. Finally, she regularly reached out by e-mail to all participants in the project to encourage them in their rituals and seek their feedback. It was clear to everyone that she took the work seriously. Her enthusiasm was infectious, and the results spoke for themselves.

At Sony Europe, several hundred leaders have embraced the principles of energy management. Over the next year, more than 2,000 of their direct reports will go through the energy renewal program. From Fujio Nishida on down, it has become increasingly culturally acceptable at Sony to take intermittent breaks, work out at midday, answer e-mail only at designated times, and even ask colleagues who seem irritable or impatient what stories they're telling themselves.

Organizational support also entails shifts in policies, practices, and cultural messages. A number of firms we worked with have built "renewal rooms" where people can regularly go to relax and refuel. Others offer subsidized gym memberships. In some cases, leaders themselves gather groups of employees for midday workouts. One company instituted a no-meeting zone between 8 and 9 AM to ensure that people had at least one hour absolutely free of meetings. At several companies, including Sony, senior leaders collectively agreed to stop checking e-mail during meetings as a way to make the meetings more fo-

A number of firms have built "renewal rooms" where people can regularly go to relax and refuel.

cused and efficient.

One factor that can get in the way of success is a crisis mentality. The optimal candidates for energy renewal programs are organizations that are feeling enough pain to be eager for new solutions but not so much that they're completely overwhelmed. At one organization where we had the active support of the CEO, the company was under intense pressure to grow rapidly, and the senior team couldn't tear themselves away from their focus on immediate survival—even though taking time out for renewal might have allowed them to be more productive at a more sustainable level.

By contrast, the group at Ernst & Young successfully went through the process at the height of tax season. With the permission of their leaders, they practiced defusing negative emotions by breathing or telling themselves different stories, and alternated highly focused periods of work with renewal breaks. Most people in the group reported that this busy season was the least stressful they'd ever experienced.

The implicit contract between organizations and their employees today is that each will try to get as much from the other as they can, as quickly as possible, and then move on without looking back. We believe that is mutually self-defeating. Both individuals and the organizations they work for end up depleted rather than enriched. Employees feel increasingly beleaguered and burned out. Organizations are forced to settle for employees who are less than fully engaged and to constantly hire and train new people to replace those who choose to leave. We envision a new and explicit contract that benefits all parties: Organizations invest in their people across all dimensions of their lives to help them build and sustain their value. Individuals respond by bringing all their multidimensional energy wholeheartedly to work every day. Both grow in value as a result.

Reprint R0710B
To order, see the next page
or call 800-988-0886 or 617-783-7500
or go to www.hbrreprints.org

Manage Your Energy, Not Your Time

Further Reading

ARTICLE
When Executives Burn Out
by Harry Levinson
Harvard Business Review
February 2000
Product no. 4290

This article describes additional ways companies can help employees replenish their personal energy. Suggestions include periodically rotating managers out of potentially exhausting positions, distributing the thorniest problems to a broad range of people rather than just to your best performers, and systematically letting people know that their contributions are important to you and the company. Levinson also recommends using pairs or teams of people to tackle tough problems so individuals won't feel isolated, training people as quickly as possible to enable them to keep up with fast-changing technologies, and maintaining personal interaction between leaders and subordinates during stressful times.

Harvard Business Review

To Order

For *Harvard Business Review* reprints and subscriptions, call 800-988-0886 or 617-783-7500. Go to www.hbrreprints.org

For customized and quantity orders of *Harvard Business Review* article reprints, call 617-783-7626, or e-mail customizations@hbsp.harvard.edu

People usually reassess their priorities only after some personal upheaval—an illness, a divorce, the loss of a job. But with the right framework, you can think through your preferences long before crisis strikes.

Do Your Commitments Match Your Convictions?

by Donald N. Sull and Dominic Houlder

Reprint R0501H

Do Your Commitments Match Your Convictions?

The Idea in Brief

How many of us struggle harder every day to uphold obligations to our bosses, families, and communities—even as the quality of our lives erodes? And how many of us feel too overwhelmed to examine the causes of this dilemma?

For most people, it takes a crisis—illness, divorce, death of a loved one, business failure—before we'll refocus our commitments of money, time, and energy on what *really* matters to us. But why wait for a crisis? Instead, use a systematic process to periodically clarify your convictions and assess whether you're putting your money (and time and energy) where your mouth is. Identify high-priority values that are receiving insufficient resources—or outdated commitments that are siphoning precious resources away from your deepest convictions.

Once you've spotted gaps between what matters most to you and how you're investing your resources, use a time-out (a sabbatical, course, or retreat) to rethink old commitments and define new ones more consistent with your values.

By routinely applying this process, you—not your past obligations—will determine the direction your life takes.

The Idea in Practice

To manage the gap between your convictions and commitments, apply the following steps.

Inventory your values.

List the things that matter most to you, in specific language. For example, instead of "Money," write, "Providing financial security to my family," or "Earning enough to retire early." Aim for five to ten values And write what you *honestly* value—not what you think you *should* value.

Assess how you're investing your resources.

Track how much money, time, and energy you're devoting to your values. For each value you've listed, record the following:

- Percentage of your household income you devote to that value

- Number of hours per week you spend on the value

- Quality of energy (high, low) you devote to activities related to that value. (An hour spent on an activity when you're fresh and focused represents a greater commitment than an hour spent when you're exhausted and distracted.)

Identify gaps between your values and commitments.

Do some values on your list receive little or none of your money, time, and energy? Is there a single value that sucks a disproportionate share of your resources away from other priorities?

Understand what has caused the gaps.

Disconnects between what you value and how you actually spend your time can have several causes. Perhaps you've taken on obligations without considering the long-term ramifications. One successful entrepreneur in New York had promised to spend more time with her London-based partner. But when she decided to sell her start-up to a West Coast competitor through a five-year earn-out deal, she had to move to San Francisco to run the business. She now spends even more time airborne—torn between two conflicting commitments she made simultaneously.

Or maybe you've let others define "success" for you. One young banker earned colleagues' praise for his extreme work ethic. When he became a father, he wanted to spend more time with his family, which baffled his colleagues. Because he badly desired continued praise from colleagues, he continued his workaholic ways—and effectively gave his colleagues the power to set his priorities.

Change course.

It's harder to recalibrate commitments when you're not facing a crisis. A time-out—a sabbatical, course, or other device—can help you reflect and give you an excuse to break old commitments and forge new ones. To avoid "commitment creep," abandon or renegotiate one old commitment for every new one you make.

People usually reassess their priorities only after some personal upheaval—an illness, a divorce, the loss of a job. But with the right framework, you can think through your preferences long before crisis strikes.

Do Your Commitments Match Your Convictions?

by Donald N. Sull and Dominic Houlder

We all hold certain things dear—professional achievement, for example, or family life, or financial security. But when we step back and take stock of our day-to-day actions, we may notice a gap between the things we value most and the way we actually spend our time, money, and attention. It may be a crevice or a chasm, but, in either case, the gap raises questions about how we manage the differences between our professed values and our actual behavior.

Consider the case of Nick, the CEO of a health care products company. (The identities of all the individuals discussed in this article have been disguised to protect their confidentiality.) He turned the organization around after it was taken private by a leveraged buyout firm and has a successful managerial track record in a range of blue-chip and entrepreneurial companies. He is highly regarded by the private-equity investors who own his parent company. But there is a huge gap between what Nick cares about and what he is actually doing. One of the best times in his

life, he told us, was when he and his wife took sabbaticals and volunteered for a year with an organization that helps immigrants—a cause that matters greatly to Nick, as the son of immigrants. He misses the time he and his wife spent together that year. "These days, given our schedules, we're lucky to spend more than one weekend a month together," he says. Nick also questions his professional impact. "At 50, I know I have five—maybe ten—good work years left," he says. "But I'm dribbling my life away working in a business that I'm not passionate about and that may or may not make me rich."

Nick is considering several career options. He could take a different CEO job; headhunters do call with offers. If his company were sold at the right price, he could retire early. He could teach at a business school. Or maybe he could work full-time at the nonprofit where he and his wife volunteered. Although Nick feels dissatisfied most days, he believes that any change must wait until he completes a major product launch at work and perhaps until he sees what happens with his equity. He says he is way too busy to do anything right now about the gap between his values and his working life. He's been "too busy" for several years running.

Perhaps your first instinct is to give Nick a thorough shaking. But the truth is, many successful people feel a similar disconnect between their daily activities and their deepest desires—and a similar inability to do anything about it. We became interested in that disconnect almost by accident. Since 1997, we have been teaching a course at London Business School on leading strategic transformations in organizations. The conceptual cornerstone of the course is commitments—the investments, public promises, contracts, and so on that bind an organization to a particular way of doing things. The course, and the research that underlies it, analyzes how historical commitments can create inertia that prevents organizations from responding effectively to changes in the competitive environment. It also explores how managers can commit to new business opportunities and thereby transform their companies.

Over the years, many of our midcareer and executive students borrowed the course's framework of commitments, inertia, and transformation and used it to think systematically about their personal and professional commitments. This happened enough times, and with enough interesting results, that we incorporated into the course a session on managing *personal* commitments. It even includes a computer-based exercise that lets students simulate personal commitments and track what kind of outcomes they may create—think the Sims discover the meaning of life. In the following pages, we'll take a closer look at this framework and describe how it can help midlife and other managers in their quest to narrow the gap between their deeply held values and their everyday activities. Let us be clear, though: We can't—and won't—try to tell you what the *content* of your personal commitments should be. We won't suggest that dedicating yourself to social service is better than making partner. Both are laudable goals. We do hope to help you improve the *process* by which you manage your personal commitments, whatever they may be.

Defining Commitments
First, let's define our terms and illustrate them in the business domain. Managerial commitments are actions taken in the present that bind an organization to a future course. When most people think of managerial commitments, they immediately call to mind dramatic actions—Boeing betting the company on the 777, for example, or Oracle acquiring PeopleSoft to build its position in applications software. In the corporate world, executives manage such commitments systematically. No responsible CEO would launch a new product or a make a major acquisition without first conducting methodical research and tracking progress against quantifiable goals. This is Business 101. Yet the most binding commitments in business are often so mundane as to be almost invisible. A company's ongoing investments in refining and extending an existing technology, for example, can cumulatively lock it onto a technological trajectory from which it is hard to escape. An organization that concentrates its sales efforts on its key customers can become dependent on those clients, limiting the firm's freedom to pursue other clients and other business options. Taken together, these kinds of mundane commitments can prove as binding as the big bets, yet they rarely receive the same level of scrutiny from managers.

A similar logic applies in our personal lives, where our most binding commitments are frequently the result of day-to-day decisions too small to attract our attention. There are exceptions, of course. Individuals periodically make dramatic commitments, such as changing jobs or getting married. And people who choose certain public-service careers, such as the military and law enforcement, may make the ultimate commitment by giving their life to a cause they believe in. For the rest of us, however, our most important commitments are the result of mundane decisions we make about how to allocate our money, time, and energy. Because these decisions are individually small, it is easy to lose sight of them, and when we do, a gap can grow between what we value and what we do.

Mind the Gap
The first step in managing your commitments is to take a quick inventory of what matters to you. (For a helpful work sheet, see the exhibit "Taking Stock.") You probably have at least a vague sense of what you value most, but it's

Donald N. Sull (dsull@london.edu) is an associate professor of management practice at London Business School. This is his fifth article for HBR. **Dominic Houlder** (dhoulder@london.edu) is the associate dean of the Sloan Fellowship program at London Business School and an executive coach.

important to clarify those themes from time to time. This exercise lets you check whether you are putting your money (and your time and energy) where your mouth is. A systematic inventory of where your money, time, and energy are going often reveals surprising gaps.

Using our work sheet, list the things that matter most to you in the first column. A few tips: It's crucial that you avoid overly vague nouns, such as "money" or "family," and instead use more specific gerunds and phrases. "Money," for example, might be articulated as "providing financial security for my family," "earning enough to retire early," or "making more than my business school section-mates." It's worth spending the time to get the language right. "Children," for example, might be broken out into a few more specific values, such as "raising well-educated, morally responsible children" or "enjoying time hanging out with my kids." These are two different values that have distinct implications for how much time you spend with your children and what activities you do with them. If you wrote the former, you might value spending time together on community service; if you wrote the latter, you might want to spend more time together at the beach. Don't be afraid to jot

down a value, scratch it out if it doesn't sound quite right, and try again until it does. There is no "right" number of values, but most people find that it takes at least five to cover the multiple dimensions of their lives (for instance, professional, family, social, religious, and individual). If the number creeps beyond ten, you're probably not focusing on the highest priority values or the most critical ones. You might want to ask your spouse or partner to do this stage of the exercise, too. You can then compare notes and explore the significance of any differences you have in what you value most. Finally, it's important to write what you honestly value rather than censoring yourself or imposing judgments about whether you should want something or not. This is not an exercise in what you (or others) *think* you should value but in what *really* matters to you.

The second step is to look closely at how committed you are, practically speaking, to the items listed in the first column. The evidence here will not be in any dramatic actions you may have taken. Such momentous events, you will recall, are comparatively rare in personal life, as they are in business. Rather, the evidence will be in the smaller, more mundane commitments we all routinely make that can

Taking Stock

WHAT MATTERS TO ME	MONEY	TIME	ENERGY
Other			

What Matters Most: A Work Sheet

Ann Montgomery is a management consultant who has been feeling some incongruity between what she values and what she actually does day to day. She used this work sheet to take inventory of her situation. She listed her values in column one and assessed how much money, time, and energy she spends on each. The percentages listed in column two represent the portions of Ann's household income that support each of her values. The hours noted in column three represent the time Ann allocates, out of total waking hours in a week, to support her stated values. And the entries in column four denote the quality of the physical and mental energy Ann devotes to her values. Values receiving her peak attention get a "+." Values receiving her attention when she's less energetic get a "-."

WHAT MATTERS TO ME	MONEY	TIME	ENERGY
Raising healthy, balanced kids; spending mostly harmonious time with family	**35%** mortgage, utilities, and home maintenance **8%** trombone lessons, soccer camp, orthodontia **12%** variable expenses—bottles of merlot, food at Trader Joe's	**15 hours** "routine"—being a taxi service, cleaning up after kids, monitoring chores **5 hours** nagging and pestering kids **5 hours** "quality"—having meaningful parent–child conversations, helping with homework	**-/+** **-** **+**
Doing interesting, useful work; gaining recognition	*Hours are up; satisfaction isn't. Why?*	**60 hours**	**+**
Saving for retirement and kids' college funds; hedging against job loss	33%	**15 minutes** worrying about Fidelity statement **15 minutes** fantasizing about Nasdaq at 10,000	**-** **++**
Spending time on activities that recharge my batteries (reading, writing, exercising, one-on-one time with friends, and vices I'm not going to admit to)	Not much—gym fees, books, merlot, occasional dinners out, treats	**5 hours** exercising **5 hours** reading **0 hours** writing	**+** **-** **-**
Maintaining close relationships—Alex (spouse), Mom, siblings, friends		**2 to 5 hours**	**-/+**
Contributing to the church—community service as well as money	2%	**0 hours** on community service	
Other	**10%** (darned if I know)	**5 to 10 hours** watching TV (worse during playoffs!), drinking merlot, reading blogs and other stuff online	**+**

Handwritten notes:
- *Time spent with kids during the week is a blur. Are we overscheduled?*
- *These always come in last…*
- *I'm really too busy right now.*

collectively lock us on a course of action. You can make the exercise concrete by taking stock of whether your daily investments of money, time, and energy are aligned with your values. Let us look at each category in turn.

Money. Over the past year, how much money have you spent on each of the values you listed? To answer this question, you can draw on the data you collect for tax purposes. "Dining out," for instance, may be a line item in your Intuit spreadsheet that jibes nicely with the value "spending time with friends." A word of warning, though: You will have to make some judgment calls. Your personal budget categories are unlikely to map directly to the values you listed. Sometimes they will not correlate at all, and the expenditures should be listed in a miscellaneous "other" category. Other times, your personal spending will map to your values in ways that aren't obvious. By taking a big mortgage on an expensive house in a tony neighborhood, for example, you also buy access to good public schools for your children. Your expenditures may correspond to more than one value, so you may want to split them across several values. You may also find that much of your money is allocated to long-term, fixed investments—a mortgage or a retirement savings account, for instance. You may prefer to assess only your discretionary spending— such as the amount you spend on memberships to health clubs or golf clubs—and leave a review of long-term investments for another time. Or you may discover that your fixed expenses—for instance, the amount you're spending on your summer home in Nantucket—are what most need to be reviewed. (By reducing your fixed costs, you also reduce the effort required to cover them, freeing up time and energy to pursue other alternatives.)

However you resolve these accounting issues, the next step is to convert the expenditures into a percentage of your household income and plot the percentages against your ranked values. (For a sample, see the exhibit "What Matters Most: A Work Sheet") Do the most important values get the most money? If not, there is evidence of a gap between values and commitments.

Time. Many people find themselves running short of time more often than they run out of money. Time is a scarce resource and one that inevitably gets depleted. By contrast, cash can increase over time if returns on investment exceed the cost of capital. In the past week, what have you done with your approximately 112 waking hours? Again, consider the values you listed, and try to map last week's hours against them. (If last week was atypical, pick the most recent week that you find representative.) As with your money, allocate only those hours that clearly support your stated values, and use the "other" category to account for the difference between total waking hours and those explicitly accounted for in your analysis. Everyone needs some downtime, of course, so you may want to include a value like "recharging my mental batteries." But also ask yourself, at what point does spending the afternoon watching college football on TV move beyond healthy rejuvenation and into the realm of wasting precious time? (Even reasonable couples may disagree on this one.) Are you dedicating the most hours to the activities that are of highest value to you? Was there a lot of time you could not account for—time that was not being used to ends that you care about?

Energy. Physical, emotional, and mental energy is another scarce resource and, like time, one that decreases with age. An hour spent on an activity when we are fresh and fully present in the moment represents a greater commitment than an hour spent when we are exhausted and distracted. Do the hours you spend with your partner, for example, generally come at the tail end of a 12-hour day and a six-day week? Was your mind plotting Monday's PowerPoint presentation during church or synagogue? On the work sheet, denote those values that, on average, receive your peak attention with a "+" and those that tend to get your least energetic focus with a "-."

Why the Gap?

Once you've filled in the work sheet as we've described, you should end up with a fair analysis of the alignment between what you value and how you commit your money, time, and energy. The basic idea is to identify big gaps— stated values that receive little or none of your scarce resources or a single value that sucks a disproportionate share of money, time, and energy from other values. If your values and your day-to-day commitments are closely aligned, we congratulate you: Many people find it difficult to strike and consistently main-

Our most binding commitments are frequently the result of day-to-day decisions too small to attract our attention.

tain this balance. Gaps between your commitments and your convictions can develop and widen with time. Understanding how these gaps can emerge is helpful in preventing them from growing too large.

Sometimes the gap results from a reluctance to commit time, energy, or money to what we value. A professional or personal failure, for instance, may shake your confidence and leave you gun-shy about making new commitments. Or perhaps you just have an innate, Peter Pan–like desire to remain in the world of potentiality for as long as possible. Of course, there are times when keeping your options open makes perfect sense. Young adults, for example, experiment with alternative careers, lifestyles, values, and relationships—which is often painful for parents to watch, generally embarrassing in retrospect, but actually a prudent discovery process.

A much more common reason for the gap is that people are entangled in commitments they made in the past. We have observed an analogous phenomenon in corporate strategy. We use the phrase "active inertia" to describe managers' tendency to respond to even the most dramatic changes in their competitive environment by relying on and accelerating activities that worked in the past. Like the driver of a car with its wheels stuck in the mud, executives notice a change in the environment and step on the gas. Ultimately, they end up digging their organizations deeper into the quagmire. The ruts that lock people into active inertia are the very commitments that led to their past successes but that have now hardened: Strategic frames become blinders, selected processes lapse into routines, relationships turn into shackles, resources become millstones, and once vibrant values ossify into dogmas.

Many of us are bound by personal commitments we willingly made in the past that no longer fit. They deplete our time, money, and energy and limit our freedom even if the commitments are no longer aligned with what we currently value. Katherine, the chief executive of a midsize nonprofit company, received an offer to run a private firm. After 20 years in social service, Katherine was attracted by the new challenge as well as the generous health care and pension package, the company car, and the higher salary, which would come in handy as she and her husband put three children through college. In the past, Katherine

had derided people who joined the for-profit world as sellouts. She and her husband, a political activist and community organizer, had consciously avoided what they considered the trappings of material life, including flashy cars, elaborate home renovations, and expensive vacations. Katherine's husband was livid when she broached the subject of taking the job, reminding her of what their friends would say. (Her husband's idealism was what had attracted Katherine to him in the first place.) Katherine's children, who had unsuccessfully pestered her for years to buy them iPods and PlayStations, accused her of hypocrisy. Although Katherine craved the financial security and new challenge, she felt trapped in a web of commitments she herself had woven.

Some of us experience "commitment creep." We often commit ourselves without really thinking about what we are taking on. It is very easy to say yes to new commitments without reflecting on the long-term costs of honoring the implied promises or the potential conflicts that may develop with existing commitments. Overcommitment is the bane of people who face many good options. Consider Hannah, a successful New York entrepreneur, who promised to spend more time with her London-based partner. Around the same time, she also received an offer from a large West Coast competitor to buy her start-up company at a juicy valuation. The deal was structured as a five-year earn-out, however, and required Hannah to move to San Francisco to run the combined business. The net result is that she is spending even more time airborne, torn between two major, conflicting commitments she made simultaneously.

The implicit nature of many professional and personal commitments also causes them to sneak up on us unnoticed. Relatively few personal commitments—marriage or religious vows among them—are explicit and public. Recall Nick, the health care CEO described earlier. His major commitment is not contractual; he has never signed an employment agreement. Rather, his sense of obligation arises from the implicit promises he made to Jerry, his company's chairman and principal investor. Nick has worked in senior roles in two of the companies Jerry bought. For more than a decade, Nick has been reinforcing an unspoken commitment to act as Jerry's right-hand man, which has now left him feeling trapped.

His reputation, identity, and stock options are as much at stake as if his commitment had been formalized.

Creeping commitments often seem especially binding because they lack the explicit boundaries and exit clauses common to legal documents. Anything you do to honor a creeping commitment will be understood as a reinforcement of an earlier promise or historical commitment—whether that is your intention or not.

Other people's expectations can also prevent us from committing our time, money, and energy to what matters most to us. Many of us measure our success against external benchmarks. Some of us remain prisoners of expectations set by our parents, long after we have left home. From childhood on, "success" means pleasing those who confer grades, jobs, prestige, and promotions. Well into adulthood, through college and graduate school, success remains a function of the esteem we receive from our peers, professors, and recruiters. In the corporate world, practices such as formal project reviews, 360-degree feedback, and annual appraisals increase our dependence on others' assessments of us.

This is fine, unless our values begin to diverge from those of our colleagues. When Ravi joined a Wall Street investment bank just out of college, for example, he cultivated a reputation for being the first in, the last out, and the hardest worker in the hours between. He relished the nickname his colleagues gave him—"the Marine." But after the birth of his first child, he wanted to spend more time with his family, which baffled his colleagues. To Ravi, it was simple: He wanted to continue to be praised for his work ethic, but he also wanted to spend more time at home. By relying on others for validation and praise, Ravi relinquished to them the power to set his priorities. As he discovered, handing the keys to others can be a problem if they're driving someplace you no longer want to go.

Moreover, some values generate less positive reinforcement than others and, as a result, tend to attract fewer resources. Consider the case of Ian, a successful director at a global management-consulting firm. During his 12 years at the company, he moved quickly through the ranks of consultant, manager, partner, and director, garnering a string of exceptional performance reviews along the way.

Although Ian highly valued the hours he spent with his family, he found that most of his time and energy were devoted to serving clients, developing junior consultants, and building the firm. When Ian examined the source of this discrepancy (ever the consultant, he used a fishbone diagram), he discovered that he had become addicted to the positive reinforcement he was getting at work—which his home life couldn't match. At the office, he explained, "my colleagues and clients respect me, and my reviews are glowing. At home, I'm lucky to get a sullen grumble from my teenage daughter and an exhausted kiss from my wife when she gets home from work." Following the principle that "what gets measured gets done," Ian began tracking the hours he spent each week with his wife and daughter and comparing his performance week after week. Ian was pleasantly surprised to find that this simple exercise focused his attention on the hours he spent at home, and the weekly comparison provided a gentle hint that he need to do more of it.

Our historical success in meeting commitments breeds the expectation—in our bosses, colleagues, friends, and family—that we will deliver more of the same. Look at Lee, a corporate tax attorney specializing in the energy industry, who is at the top of her profession. She chairs prestigious committees, publishes in leading journals, and attracts high-profile clients who want her advice on thorny issues. Lee has always loved a professional challenge—in fact, her desire to seek out and solve the hard problems has driven her success. But after 25 years in the field, Lee told us, she had become increasingly bored with her work and longed for the intellectual excitement that characterized the early part of her career. She was reluctant, however, to scale back her lifestyle. Perhaps more important, the prospect of tackling a completely new endeavor—at age 50, no less—seemed daunting to her. "I almost wish I hadn't been so successful in law," she told us, "because then I wouldn't feel like I had so much to lose if I fell flat on my face trying something new."

The penny dropped at her 25th law school reunion. One-hundred or so of her contemporaries were all benchmarking themselves against one another. The inevitable success stories—Lee was telling them, too—were like spells that she now wanted to break. She realized she was feeling unfulfilled in part because of the company she was keeping: She worked all day with the lawyers and staffers in her firm. And because much of her time outside work was spent on professional service, she associated with many of the same attorneys on evenings and weekends. During her reunion, Lee recognized that her concerns about maintaining her current lifestyle had a lot to do with her wanting to keep up with her peers. To make a change, Lee cultivated friendships with acquaintances outside her immediate circle who sympathized with her aspiration to do something new and had themselves made major career shifts. She also cut in half the amount of time she spent attending professional conferences.

Changing Course

Most people who undertake the self-exploration process we're describing here find that it's relatively easy to identify their own values, somewhat more difficult to analyze the gap between their values and the way they actually live, and harder still to analyze the reasons for this gap. But the hardest task of all is doing something about *closing* the gap. As we know from organizational life, change is very easy to talk about and extremely difficult to pull off. The force of inertia is every bit as powerful in our personal lives as it is in most organizations.

The most common catalyst for serious change is a personal or professional crisis, such as the death of a loved one, a personal illness, a business failure, the loss of a job, or a divorce. No one wishes for crises; they drain not just money, time, and energy but often health, confidence and reputation. But crises do push some people to deliberately reexamine their commitments.

Annette was an independent consultant who worked within a network. Although she was putting in more and more hours, she found that she was spending less and less time on projects that really engaged her imagination and advanced her skills. She was trapped by layers of old commitments, some of which had crept up on her unnoticed. Never wanting to disappoint a client, she invariably delivered excellent work, on time. Her clients and colleagues expected more and more of the same. Years of professional success had left Annette with little freedom to devote herself to the things she really cared about.

Then her mother was diagnosed with terminal cancer, and Annette's priorities changed. At the top of her list was ensuring that her mother got the best possible care. Next was spending quality time with her mother in her final months. Further down the list were her commitments to clients and associates; in many cases, those commitments had to be abandoned. Annette's mother's illness lasted for six months and, like any crisis, consumed considerable time, energy, and money. But it also created advantages both obvious and unforeseen. Specifically:

Crises force people to figure out what really matters. In the end, all crises are reminders that we are not omnipotent or immortal and that we cannot afford to ignore the things that really matter to us. Her mother's illness and death sent a message to Annette: She had to make the most of her own life. That meant committing herself only to those professional projects she found interesting and challenging—not entering into the same kinds of engagements with the same kinds of clients using the same kinds of PowerPoint presentations where only the names change. It also meant spending more time with the people who mattered to her most, including her equally harried partner and her estranged father.

Crises force people to make choices. While some people fail to commit because they feel trapped by promises they've already made, others simply avoid making commitments altogether. A crisis will often demolish our commitment-avoidance strategies. The loss of a job, or an unexpected denial of promotion, can be the catalyst for exploring what we really want to make of our working lives.

Crises can nullify outdated commitments. A crisis in one's personal life is analogous to a force majeure contract clause in a legal document—all previous promises are nullified because of unanticipated or uncontrollable events. The people to whom Annette had previously committed her time and energy, for instance, understood that caring for her mother took precedence over earlier claims on Annette's resources. The slate was clean.

Crises prompt people to clear their diaries. During the six months that Annette was home caring for her mother, she had handed over most of her clients to colleagues, leaving her with a largely empty calendar. That allowed her to rebuild her professional life step by step, taking on new commitments.

Crises help to break the cycle of success. We noted earlier that many successful people feel trapped by their very success. A failure in the workplace, while undoubtedly painful, can also be liberating. Once you and the people around you see that you failed, but that the failure neither killed you nor destroyed your many strengths, it becomes easier to change direction and take on new challenges. When Annette returned to the workplace and began to remake her commitments, she focused on creative and stretch assignments rather than leaning on old ways of doing things.

It's harder (and braver) to make new commitments and rethink old ones when we are not facing a crisis. Which is why time-outs—sabbaticals, executive education courses, or any other catalyst for breaking the thread of a narrative—are so important. Such breaks confer some of the benefits of a crisis—particularly some time to reflect, an excuse to break old commitments, and a chance to clear the diary—without exacting the high costs. That being said, it would be wrong to suggest that changing direction is easy, even if you're reasonably certain about where you want to go. People tend to encounter the following pitfalls when attempting to remake their commitments.

The Great Leap Forward. Some people end up making unrealistic commitments that are bound to fail—great leaps that cannot be made. These commitments can be very enticing; they're novel and exciting for a while. But they are also very risky. Such commitments can provide an excuse for failing to make or keep more mundane commitments. Members of Alcoholics Anonymous, for instance, are discouraged from pledging that they will never drink again; they are encouraged to take it one day at a time. Or consider Maria, a Brazilian who received her undergraduate and MBA degrees in the United States and stayed to work as a marketing executive in a large consumer goods company in the Midwest. After more than 15 years in the States, she was anxious to spend more time with her aging parents in São Paulo. She quit her job and moved to Brazil without lining up a new position. Although she enjoyed spending more time with her parents, she was deeply frustrated by her inability

to find a position of comparable responsibility with a world-class company. And she missed the United States and her friends more than she had imagined. Two companies and 18 months later, Maria decided to return to the United States and concluded that she would have been better served by taking a one-year posting in Brazil with a multinational to test the waters professionally and personally.

The Go-It-Alone Fallacy. Remaking historical commitments is not a solo sport; after all, these are promises others rely on. Social organizations—families, churches, companies, and communities, for instance—are held together by the promises embedded in individual members' commitments. Undoing these commitments can disrupt organizations and undermine individuals' credibility. As the world changes around us or as our values evolve, we need to renegotiate existing commitments with those who would be affected by these changes, not try to make unilateral moves. For example, Susan, a high-powered London-based executive, wants to scale back her professional obligations to spend more time with her preschool-aged children. To do so, she would need to talk with her boss and her colleagues about how to reduce and restructure her workload. Even more daunting, in Susan's eyes, is the prospect of discussing with her husband, Donald, how this change in commitments would affect their family and financial responsibilities as well as the couple's overall lifestyle. Most important, she wonders, who would get to make the final decision?

The Clutter Trap. We fall into this trap when we are not systematically undoing old commitments as we take on new ones. As a result, so many promises—new and old—call out for our time and other resources that we may meet none of them or simply fall back on what we were doing before. Many of us have experienced this in our professional lives when we attend management meetings that add new items to our to-do list without removing existing ones. Taken as a whole, the agenda that emerges can be impossible. Let us look at Margaret, a senior executive in a large European firm, who realized she couldn't make new commitments to what she knew had to be done because of existing clutter. She had objectives for more than 50 different key performance indicators at work. Scrambling to achieve those objectives prevented her from taking on new ones. A good rule of thumb for avoiding clutter is to abandon or renegotiate an old commitment for every new one you make. Margaret, for example, scheduled an hour a month to cull her diary, canceling meetings as higher priorities arose.

• • •

The final assignment in the course we teach on leading strategic change in organizations invites students to state the commitments they will make (or remake) after the program ends. We are always struck by the diversity of approaches that different students take to this assignment, even after sitting in the same classroom for a semester. This is why we are not offering you hard-and-fast rules for mak-

ing or remaking your commitments. No such formula is possible for a process that is, by its very nature, highly idiosyncratic and dependent on individual circumstances. But you can manage the gap between what you value and what you do by periodically and systematically reexamining your values and the way you allocate precious resources. Such an exercise can help you take control of your future commitments so that past commitments won't take control of you.

Reprint R0501H
To order, see the next page
or call 800-988-0886 or 617-783-7500
or go to www.hbr.org

Do Your Commitments Match Your Convictions?

Further Reading

A R T I C L E
Managing by Commitments
by Donald N. Sull
Harvard Business Review
June 2003
Product no. R0306E

Sull urges us to apply the same thoughtfulness to professional commitments as we do to personal commitments. Your professional commitments—R&D investments, public promises to hit growth targets, hiring decisions—set your business's direction. They each involve actions you take *today* that bind your company to a course of action *tomorrow*.

Commitments also shape your business's identity—establishing opportunities and limitations, and focusing and energizing employees. But like double-edged swords, they can be dangerous if made carelessly. While each decision defines your company's capabilities now, it also reduces its flexibility in the future. When competitive conditions change, you may be unable to respond effectively.

You can't anticipate every commitment's long-term consequences, but you shouldn't shy away from making commitments. How to wield these double-edged swords? Before each key decision, ask, "Am I locking us into a course of action we'll regret later?" When disruptive change strikes, let go of "business as usual" in favor of *transforming* commitments—investing in revamped processes and new resources, establishing new partnerships, and defining new values.